CHINESE COOKBOOK

Cover
Crisp Fried Pork with Sweet Sour Sauce (See page 76)

Frontispiece
Heavenly Braised Vegetables (See page 89)

Frontispiece opposite
Barbecue Style Roast Duck (See page 61)

First published 1973 by
Paul Hamlyn Pty Limited
Reprinted 1974, 1975
First U.S. edition published 1976 by
The Tradewinds Group
176 South Creek Road,
Dee Why West, NSW, Australia, 2099
© Paul Hamlyn Pty Limited 1973, 1976
Printed in Hong Kong

ISBN   0   909163   01   4

CHINESE COOKBOOK

CHARMAINE SOLOMON

Photographer Reg Morrison

TRADEWINDS

SYDNEY • AUCKLAND • LONDON • NEW YORK • TORONTO

CONTENTS

GUIDE TO WEIGHTS AND MEASURES 9
EQUIVALENT MEASURES 10
INGREDIENTS
  EQUIVALENTS OR SUBSTITUTES 10
TERMS AND EQUIPMENT 11
UTENSILS FOR CHINESE COOKING 12
SOUPS 15
SEAFOOD 32
POULTRY AND EGGS 49
PORK AND BEEF 65
VEGETABLES 84
RICE AND NOODLES 93
SNACKS, SAUCES AND SWEETS 105
GLOSSARY 130
INDEX 133

Introduction

Chinese food has always been part of my life.

I grew up in Eastern countries with sizable Chinese populations and the opportunity to know good Chinese food. To help matters along, the man I married turned out to be really keen on Chinese food . . . not just eating it, but cooking it. He would pursue recipes with the singlemindedness of a bloodhound and so it came about that between us we learned a great deal about a cuisine neither of us was born into.

The cuisine of China is acknowledged as one of the world's greatest, yet Chinese food is extremely simple to cook. There are no complex sauces, no tricky techniques, no mysterious procedures that need a master chef to explain. Anyone really interested can learn from simply expressed recipes, the cooking methods and distinctive seasonings, and turn out wonderful Oriental dishes in a Western kitchen.

I hope that through this book you, too, will discover the joys of cooking and eating Chinese food.

Guide to weights and measures

A special note to American readers

Two systems of measurement for recipe ingredients have been used side by side throughout this book. As an example:

Ingredients	Metric	Imperial
Whole snapper	750 g	1 ½ lb
Water	185 ml	¾ cup

American Standard measures are exactly the same as the 'Imperial' measures as used in this book, **except that** the 'Imperial' pint has a capacity of 20 fluid ounces (two and a half 8 fl oz cups) whereas the American Standard pint has a capacity of 16 fluid ounces (two 8 fl oz cups).

It must be stressed that the quantities given in the American ('Imperial') and Metric ingredients listings are in proportion, but they are NOT exact conversions — the Metric yield is approximately 10 per cent greater than the equivalent American Standard yield. Therefore, to use this book successfully,

follow AMERICAN STANDARD quantities

or

follow METRIC quantities

but

do **NOT** use a mixture of the two.

Using Metric measures

The Metric measuring cup specified in this book has a capacity of **250 millilitres** (250 ml). Clearly graduated Metric measuring cups and jugs can therefore be used for all liquid and dry cup quantities given in the recipes. Note that:

¼ Metric cup	=	60 ml		
½ Metric cup	=	125 ml		
¾ Metric cup	=	185 ml		
1 Metric cup	=	250 ml	=	¼ litre
2 Metric cups	=	500 ml	=	½ litre
3 Metric cups	=	750 ml	=	¾ litre
4 Metric cups	=	1,000 ml	=	1 litre

The American Standard teaspoon and tablespoon can be used for measuring Metric quantities. The American teaspoon has exactly the same capacity as the Metric teaspoon specified in this book:

1 Metric teaspoon = 5 ml = 1 American teaspoon

The American tablespoon is fractionally smaller than the Metric tablespoon specified in this book. Therefore, use a generous American Standard tablespoon when using it for Metric quantities:

1 Metric tablespoon = 20 ml = 1 ⅓ American tablespoons

Equivalent Measures

Most ingredients that are weighed in Australia are measured by volume (cups, tablespoons, teaspoons) in America. The following list gives approximate equivalent measures for such ingredients used in this book.

Ingredient	'Imperial' weight	American Standard measure
bean sprouts, fresh	2 oz	1 cup
broccoli, sliced	4 oz	1 cup
chestnuts, dried	4 oz	1 cup
crab meat	6 oz	1 cup
lard	8 oz	1 cup
	4 oz	½ cup
	2 oz	¼ cup
	1 oz	2 tablespoons
meat, raw ground	8 oz	1 cup
mushrooms	4 oz	1 cup
scallops, shucked	8 oz	1 cup
shrimps, shucked	6 oz	1 cup

Ingredients — Equivalents or Substitutes
(see also Glossary, pages 130-132)

Australian	American
almond essence	almond extract
belly pork	fresh pork side
bicarbonate of soda	baking soda
bream	sole
capsicums	sweet or bell peppers
castor sugar	fine granulated sugar
chump (lamb)	leg steaks
cornflour	cornstarch
dessicated coconut	shredded coconut
Epsom salts	magnesium sulfate
fillet (of meat)	tenderloin
gravy beef	stew beef
jewfish	halibut
king prawns	jumbo shrimps, scampi
mince/minced (meat)	ground

Australian	American
plain flour	all-purpose flour
prawns	shrimps
rasher (of bacon)	slice
rump steak	sirloin
Scotch fillet	sirloin
shallots	scallions
shin (of meat)	shank
snow peas	sugar peas, mange-tout
tomato sauce	tomato catsup

Terms and Equipment

absorbent kitchen paper	paper towels
biscuits	cookies
frying pan	skillet
grill	broil/broiler
(to) shell	(to) shuck, hull

Utensils for Chinese cooking

Almost every Chinese dish can be prepared in a Western kitchen using Western equipment. But if you are keen on cooking Chinese food and want to buy special utensils, here is a guide to the most useful.

THE WOK

If I had to choose one cooking pan to be marooned on a desert island with, I'd choose a wok! It would cope with any kind of food that happened to be available.

If you want to cook Chinese style, I would urge you to buy a wok before you even start to cook your first Chinese meal because it makes everything so much easier. It is truly an all-purpose cooking utensil. In it you boil, braise, fry and steam. But while you can do all these things in pans you already possess, the wok is almost indispensable for the stir-frying technique that many Chinese dishes call for.

You may, of course, use a large, deep frying pan, but I have cooked stir-fried dishes in a deep frying pan, side by side with a wok, and I say without hesitation that the wok's a winner every time. Because of its spherical shape and high, flaring sides you can toss with abandon and stir-fry ingredients without their leaping over the sides. And because it is made of thin iron you get the quick, high heat so necessary in Chinese cooking. With one you can do anything and everything the recipes in this book require and achieve the best results.

Don't feel you've got to pay a lot and buy a stainless steel wok. Modestly priced iron woks are the best. They heat up more quickly and evenly and if you remember to dry them well after washing, they will not rust. The handles get rather hot, but I've found that winding 2 or 3 layers of insulating tape around them keeps the handles quite comfortable to hold. The 12 in — 13 in size wok is the most useful.

TO SEASON YOUR WOK

An iron wok must be prepared before it is used by washing thoroughly with hot water and detergent. Some woks, when new, have a lacquer-like coating and this must be removed by almost filling the wok with water, adding about 2 tablespoons bicarbonate of soda, and boiling for about 15 minutes. This softens the coating and it may be scrubbed off with a fine scourer. If some of the coating still remains, repeat the process until the wok is free from any coating on the inside. Now season the wok. Dry well, place over gentle heat, then wipe over the entire inside surface with a wad of absorbent kitchen paper dipped in peanut oil. Repeat with more oil-soaked paper until paper remains clean. Allow to cool. Your wok is now ready for use.

After use, do not scrub the wok with steel wool or abrasives. Soak to soften any remaining food, rub gently with a sponge or dish mop, using hot water and detergent. This preserves the surface. And make sure the wok is quite dry because if moisture is left in the pan it will rust. A well used wok will soon turn black, but this is normal. And the more a wok is used, the better it is to cook in.

CHINESE CHOPPER

The Chinese chopper or cleaver may look clumsy to the uninitiated, but is the best thing for slicing, shredding, chopping, dicing. As an extra bonus, its wide blade about 9 cm (3½-inches) across and twice that in length, can be used to transport cut up ingredients from chopping block to cooking pan. Use it on a wooden block or board. I do not recommend laminated chopping boards, whatever kind of knife you use. Young homemakers often succumb to their attractive appearance, but when you get down to serious cooking there's nothing to take the place of a solid wooden chopping block.

STEAMERS

The Chinese use steamers of aluminium or bamboo, but these are not essential. Steaming may be done in any covered pot large enough to accommodate a plate placed on a rack or a bowl to hold it well above the level of the water. The plate should be of a size which will allow free circulation of steam around and above it. The food to be cooked is placed on the plate, the pot covered with a well fitting lid, and there you have a perfectly adequate improvised steamer.

For steaming buns or dumplings, however, use a perforated

rack or colander placed on top of a pan of boiling water. Cover with a clean cloth and then a lid. This prevents steam gathering on the lid and falling back onto the buns. The Chinese bamboo steamers which are placed over a wok half filled with water are particularly suitable as the natural perforations on the lid allow excess steam to escape and makes them ideal for cooking dim sim and pau.

OTHER KITCHEN AIDS

Chinese ladles and frying spoons are useful, but not strictly necessary, if you have other utensils that will do the job. Any kind of ladle may be used for dipping out stock and I have found that the curved, slotted spatula available so cheaply from chain stores or hardware departments, is ideal for tossing and stir-frying. It is supposed to crush, strain, whip and lift and, if the makers only knew, is ideal for stir-frying as well.

For deep frying, the Chinese wire frying spoons are useful. A medium to large size spoon can cope with a whole fish, lifting it out of the oil with ease, which is a consideration if you like deep fried whole fish.

Long wooden cooking chopsticks are also useful, especially for separating noodles as they cook, and for a variety of other jobs too.

soups

When I was a very little girl, my mother was invited by wealthy Chinese friends to a formal banquet of innumerable courses, of which bird's nest soup was one. For a long time I was fascinated at the idea of tiny swallows spinning nests on almost inaccessible cliffs and these nests being used to make soup.

It was quite some years later that I too attended a Chinese meal of sufficient importance to include this soup on the menu. Because the main ingredients are costly and days of preparation are involved, bird's nest soup and shark's fin soup are served as prestige courses at banquets. But most Chinese soups are simply and easily made.

Well flavoured stock provides the basis for the bowls of fragrant goodness that send many Westerners crowding into Chinese restaurants during the lunch hour to have a bowl of soup, even if there is no time for anything more. And indeed, a combination soup is a meal in itself. Some of the soups in this chapter are simple, while others need a little more preparation. Use these recipes as a starting point and create your own favourite combinations.

Once you have made the stock (see basic stock recipes) you can add any meat, seafood, poultry, vegetables or noodles you have on hand for a delicious one-dish meal. But do pay attention to the seasonings, even if the quantities seem hardly worth worrying about. "One star anise", "a slice of fresh ginger" or "a few drops of sesame oil" may not seem much, but therein lies the whole difference between your delicately flavoured Chinese dish and just another bowl of soup.

Basic chicken stock

Ingredients	Metric	Imperial
Chicken bones and trimmings (giblets, neck, feet, etc.)		
Cold water	1.5 litres	6 cups
Peppercorns	10	10
Celery with leaves	2 small stalks	2 small stalks
Onion	1	1
Coriander or parsley stalks	3 or 4	3 or 4
Fresh root ginger	2 slices	2 slices
Salt	to taste	to taste

Put bones and trimmings in a saucepan, add water and other ingredients, bring to the boil. Cover and simmer 45 minutes to 1 hour. Strain. Skim if necessary. The stock is now ready for use in soups and sauces.

Basic beef stock

Ingredients	Metric	Imperial
Soup bones	1 kg	2 lb
Gravy beef	500 g	1 lb
Cold water	2 litres	8 cups
Onion	1	1
Celery with leaves	1 stalk	1 stalk
Star anise	1	1
Coriander or parsley stalks	4	4
Salt	3 teaspoons	3 teaspoons

Put bones and beef into a large pan with water to cover. Add all other ingredients. Bring to the boil, then cover and simmer for 2 hours. Strain and allow to cool, then chill. Remove fat from surface. Use as a base for soup or as part of the liquid in sauces for beef, chicken or pork dishes.

Basic fish stock

Ingredients	Metric	Imperial
Fish heads and trimmings or prawn heads and shells	as available	as available
Cold water	2 litres	8 cups
Peppercorns	10	10
Fresh root ginger	3 slices	3 slices
Carrot	1	1
Celery	2 stalks	2 stalks
Onion	1 large	1 large
Coriander	2 stalks	2 stalks

Wash fish trimmings, prawn heads and shells thoroughly. Put into a large pan with cold water to cover, add remaining ingredients and bring to the boil. Cover and simmer 1 hour or longer. Strain stock and use in soups or as part of the liquid in seafood dishes.

Whole chicken soup

Serves: 4-5

Ingredients	Metric	Imperial
Chicken	1 kg	2 lb
Cold water		
Rice	250 g	1 cup
Salt	2 teaspoons	2 teaspoons
Five-spice powder	½ teaspoon	½ teaspoon
Celery, sliced	1 stalk	1 stalk
Onion, sliced	1	1

Put whole chicken into a large saucepan with sufficient cold water to completely cover it. Wash rice in 3 or 4 changes of water, drain, add to pan. Add salt, five-spice, celery and onion, bring to the boil, then simmer, covered, for 1½ hours or until rice is very soft. If necessary, add more boiling water during cooking time.

Serve soup first, then serve chicken, which should be tender enough to break with chopsticks. With the chicken, serve dipping sauces. (See page 122).

Pork and Prawn Ball Soup with Bamboo Shoot (See page 24)

Chicken and asparagus soup

Serves: 4-5

Ingredients	Metric	Imperial
Chicken stock	2 litres	8 cups
Chicken breast	1	1
Asparagus pieces	1 small can	1 small can
Cornflour	3 teaspoons	3 teaspoons
Cold water	2 tablespoons	2 tablespoons
Chinese wine or sherry	1 tablespoon	1 tablespoon
Eggs, beaten	2	2

Make stock according to recipe on page 16 or use chicken stock cubes. Cut flesh from chicken breast into small dice. Set aside. Drain asparagus pieces, reserving liquid. Combine stock and liquid from asparagus, add diced chicken and bring to the boil. Lower heat, simmer 5 minutes, then add cornflour mixed with cold water and return to the boil, stirring until soup thickens slightly.

Add wine or sherry, slowly dribble in the beaten eggs, stirring. Add asparagus pieces, heat through and serve.

Chicken velvet and sweet corn soup

Chicken velvet is the name given to a purée made from chicken meat (usually white meat from the breast). This is minced or very finely chopped so it is smooth in texture. The delicate golden soup combines the chicken puree with creamed corn.

Serves: 4-5

Ingredients	Metric	Imperial
Chicken breast	1 large	1 large
Salt	½ teaspoon	½ teaspoon
Cold water	2 tablespoons	2 tablespoons
Chicken stock	1.25 litres	5 cups
Creamed corn	1 x 250 g can	1 x 8 oz can
Cornflour	1½ tablespoons	1½ tablespoons
Sesame oil	1 teaspoon	1 teaspoon
Chinese wine or sherry	2 tablespoons	2 tablespoons
Smoked ham or bacon	2 thin slices	2 thin slices

Bone the chicken breast. Use the bone, a stalk of celery, an onion and a slice of ginger to make the stock. Or use chicken stock cubes. Remove skin from chicken and very finely chop the flesh until it is almost a paste. Add the salt and water to it, mixing well. Mix corn and chicken together. Strain chicken stock into a saucepan, bring to the boil, add the chicken mixture.

Bring slowly to the boil again, then stir in cornflour mixed with a little cold water. Return to boil, stirring, and cook until thickened, about 1 minute. Stir in sesame oil and wine or sherry.

Serve at once, sprinkled with the finely chopped ham.

Pork and cabbage soup

Serves: 6

Ingredients	Metric	Imperial
Pork bones	1 kg	2 lb
Five-spice powder	½ teaspoon	½ teaspoon
Fresh root ginger, finely grated	½ teaspoon	½ teaspoon
Garlic, crushed	1 clove	1 clove
Salt	1 teaspoon	1 teaspoon
Cornflour	3 teaspoons	3 teaspoons
Cold water	2 tablespoons	2 tablespoons
Chinese wine or dry sherry	1 tablespoon	1 tablespoon
Barbecued pork fillet (see page 79)	250 g	8 oz
Chinese cabbage, finely sliced	750 g	3 cups

Put bones with five-spice powder, ginger and garlic into a saucepan, add 2 litres (8 cups) water and bring to the boil. Cover and simmer for 1½-2 hours.

Strain stock, return to boil, add cornflour mixed with water. Boil for 3 minutes, then add sherry, barbecued pork cut in thin slices, and the cabbage. Return to boil and boil for 1 minute. Stir well and serve.

Pork and prawn ball soup with bamboo shoot

Serves: 6

Ingredients	Metric	Imperial
Pork balls:		
Pork mince	500 g	1 lb
Fresh root ginger, finely grated	¼ teaspoon	¼ teaspoon
Garlic, crushed	1 clove	1 clove
Salt	1 teaspoon	1 teaspoon
Shallots, finely chopped	2 tablespoons	2 tablespoons
Prawn balls:		
Raw prawns	500 g	1 lb
Fresh root ginger, finely grated	¼ teaspoon	¼ teaspoon
Salt	½ teaspoon	½ teaspoon
Soft white bread, crumbed	1 slice	1 slice
Egg yolk	1	1
Cornflour	1 teaspoon	1 teaspoon
Soup:		
Pork or chicken stock	1.5 litres	6 cups
Chinese wine or dry sherry	1 tablespoon	1 tablespoon
Canned bamboo shoot, sliced	3 tablespoons	3 tablespoons
Cornflour	3 teaspoons	3 teaspoons
Cold water	2 tablespoons	2 tablespoons
Sesame oil	½ teaspoon	½ teaspoon
Shallots, finely chopped	2 tablespoons	2 tablespoons

Pork balls: Combine all ingredients, form into balls the size of a large marble. Bring stock to the boil, drop in balls and bamboo shoot and return to the boil. Simmer for 15 minutes. Meanwhile make prawn balls.

Prawn balls: Shell and de-vein prawns and chop very finely. Combine with all other ingredients, form into balls the same size as the pork balls and drop into simmering stock after pork balls have cooked 15 minutes. Return to simmering point, cook for a further 7 minutes. (This recipe is not successful with cooked prawns.)

Stir in Chinese wine or dry sherry, then the cornflour mixed with the cold water. Boil, stirring until soup is clear and slightly thickened, about 1 minute. Stir in sesame oil. Serve, garnished with finely chopped shallots.

Egg flower soup

Serves: 4-5

This simple, nourishing soup can be made in a few minutes, using chicken stock cubes. The beaten egg will set when poured into the boiling soup and look like chrysanthemum petals.

Serves: 4-5

Chicken stock	1 litre	4 cups
Chinese wine or dry sherry	2 tablespoons	2 tablespoons
Sesame oil	1 teaspoon	1 teaspoon
Salt	to taste	to taste
Eggs, beaten slightly	3	3
Shallots, chopped	3 tablespoons	3 tablespoons

Bring stock to the boil, add sherry and sesame oil. Taste and add more salt if necessary.

Season beaten eggs with ½ teaspoon salt, pour slowly into the boiling soup. Stir once or twice. Serve at once, sprinkled with chopped shallots.

Crab and egg soup

I remember a Chinese restaurant in Colombo which specialised in this soup. Their chef made it with fresh crab and it was a soup to remember. But canned or frozen crab meat may be substituted if fresh crab is difficult to obtain.
Serves: 5-6

Ingredients	Metric	Imperial
Crab	1 large	1 large
Fish or chicken stock	1.5 litres	6 cups
Eggs, slightly beaten	4	4
Cornflour	2 tablespoons	2 tablespoons
Cold water	4 tablespoons	4 tablespoons
Shallots, finely sliced	6	6

If using fresh crab, cook in water with seasoning as for fish stock for 10 minutes, cool, then pick out flesh and reserve. Discard shell and fibrous tissue from stomach. Flake crab meat, discarding any bony tissue.

Bring stock to the boil. Slowly dribble in the beaten eggs. Stir gently. After 2 minutes stir in the cornflour mixed smoothly with the cold water, return soup to the boil and stir constantly until it is clear and slightly thickened.

Add crab meat and heat through. Serve immediately, sprinkled with shallots.

Prawn and mushroom soup

Serves: 4-5

Ingredients	Metric	Imperial
Raw prawns	500 g	1 lb
Sesame oil	1 tablespoon	1 tablespoon
Rice	½ metric cup	½ cup
*Chinese soup greens (gai choy) chopped	1 metric cup	1 cup
Braised mushrooms (see page 90)	8	8
Salt	to taste	to taste

Shell prawns, reserving heads and shells. De-vein prawns and cut into halves or, if large, into quarters. Wash the heads and shells thoroughly, drain in a colander. Heat oil in a saucepan, throw in the prawn heads and shells and fry over high heat, stirring until they turn pink. Then add boiling water to cover (approximately 2 litres (8 cups), cover pan with lid and simmer for 30 minutes. Strain, discard heads and shells.

Make up prawn stock to 1.5 litres (6 cups) with water, return to saucepan and add rice and 2 teaspoons salt, cover and simmer 1 hour or longer, until rice is very soft.

Chop cabbage into bite sized pieces. Cut mushrooms into thin slices. Add mushrooms to soup together with prawns. Simmer for 5 minutes, add more salt if necessary, then add cabbage. Simmer 1 minute longer. Serve at once.

Note: This recipe may be made with mushrooms which have not been braised. In this case soak them in hot water for 30 minutes, remove and discard stems and slice mushroom caps finely. Add to soup at the same time as rice, and finish the soup with a few drops of sesame oil and a teaspoon of soy sauce.

*Any variety of Chinese soup vegetables may be used in this soup, but if you ask for "gai choy" in a Chinese shop, you will be given the one I have used in this recipe. It looks like a small variety of Chinese mustard cabbage and has the same slightly pungent flavour.

Short soup (wonton soup)

Serves: 4

Ingredients	Metric	Imperial
Raw prawns	60 g	2 oz
Minced pork	125 g	4 oz
Shallots, chopped	2	2
Salt	½ teaspoon	½ teaspoon
Soy sauce	1 tablespoon	1 tablespoon
Garlic, crushed	1 clove	1 clove
Fresh root ginger, finely grated	¼ teaspoon	¼ teaspoon
Wonton wrappers	125 g	4 oz
Chicken stock	1 litre	4 cups
Sesame oil	few drops	few drops
Shallots or fresh coriander, finely chopped	3 tablespoons	3 tablespoons

Shell and de-vein prawns and chop finely. Mix together prawns, pork, shallots, salt, soy sauce, garlic and ginger.

Place a small amount of the meat filling on each square of noodle dough and fold in two diagonally, moistening edges and pressing together. Then fold one corner across and stick to the first fold. Do the same with the other corner. The three ends of the triangle should be distinct for soup wonton.

Drop into the boiling stock, return to the boil and cook for about 7 minutes. Turn off heat, add sesame oil, sprinkle with shallots or coriander and serve at once.

Variation:

Short soup with vegetables

Serves: 5-6

Ingredients	Metric	Imperial
Chicken stock	1.5 litres	6 cups
Short soup dumplings (see Wonton soup (above)		

Snow peas	30 g	1 oz
Broccoli sprigs	1 metric cup	1 cup
Chinese parsley, finely chopped	2 tablespoons	2 tablespoons
Sesame oil	few drops	few drops

Bring chicken stock (made with cubes) to the boil and drop the dumplings in. Cook for 8 minutes. Add the peas and broccoli and cook for 2-3 minutes longer. Remove from heat, stir in parsley and sesame oil and serve at once.

Combination soup

Use any combination of meat and vegetables.

Serves: 4-6

Ingredients	Metric	Imperial
Chicken, lean pork or beef	250 g	8 oz
Water	1.5 litres	6 cups
Garlic	1 clove	1 clove
Fresh root ginger	2 slices	2 slices
Celery	1 stalk	1 stalk
Salt	2 teaspoons	2 teaspoons
Cooked prawns	125 g	4 oz
Chinese cabbage, sliced	3 metric cups	3 cups
Shallots, cut in 5 cm lengths (2 inch) lengths	3	3
Sesame oil	few drops	few drops

Cut pork or beef into thin slices. If using chicken, use wings or thighs for preference.

Place meat in a suacepan, add water, garlic, celery and salt and bring to the boil. Cover and simmer for 30 minutes. Remove ginger and garlic and discard.

If chicken thighs or other large joints are used, remove flesh from bones, cut and dice. Discard bones.

Add prawns and vegetables, return to the boil for 1 minute, sitr in sesame oil and serve.

Combination long soup

A bowl of this soup can be a complete meal. It gets its unusual name from the long strands of noodles, usually fresh noodles, which are a main ingredient. Add meats and vegetables as available.

Serves: 6

Ingredients	Metric	Imperial
Chinese mushrooms, soaked and cut in strips	6	6
Eggs, beaten	2	2
Salt		
Pepper		
Sesame oil	few drops	few drops
Fine egg noodles	250 g	8 oz
Chicken stock (or water and stock cubes)	2 litres	8 cups
Lean pork or chicken	250 g	8 oz
Peanut oil	2 tablespoons	2 tablespoons
Garlic, bruised	1 clove	1 clove
Fresh root ginger	2 slices	2 slices
Chinese cabbage cut in strips	3 metric cups	3 cups
Canned bamboo shoot, diced	1	1
Soy sauce	2 tablespoons	2 tablespoons
Chinese wine or sherry	2 tablespoons	2 tablespoons
Salt	to taste	to taste
Sesame oil	1 teaspoon	1 teaspoon

Soak dry mushrooms in hot water for 30 minutes, discard stems and slice mushrooms finely

Season eggs with a little salt and pepper. Heat an omelette pan, grease lightly with a few drops of sesame oil, and pour in half the beaten egg to make a thin omelette. Repeat with remaining egg. Slice finely and set aside.

Cook noodles for 2 minutes in plenty of lightly salted boiling water. Drain in colander and run cold water through to separate. Drain again. Heat chicken stock.

Shred pork or chicken very finely. Heat peanut oil in a wok, fry garlic and ginger and discard when they are brown. Add pork or chicken to the flavoured oil, fry quickly, stirring, until colour changes. Add vegetables, fry 2 minutes longer.

Add fried mixture and noodles to chicken stock, return to the boil. Add soy sauce, sherry and salt to taste. Stir in sesame oil. Serve immediately, garnished with omelette strips.

Long soup with king prawns

Serves: 5-6

Ingredients	Metric	Imperial
Large raw prawns	500 g	1 lb
Chinese dried mushrooms	8	8
Fine egg noodles	250 g	8 oz
Fish or prawn stock	1.5 litres	6 cups
Salt	to taste	to taste
Chinese cabbage, shredded	3 metric cups	3 cups
Sesame oil	1 teaspoon	1 teaspoon
Peanut oil	2 tablespoons	2 tablespoons
Garlic, crushed	1 clove	1 clove
Fresh root ginger, finely grated	½ teaspoon	½ teaspoon
Soy sauce	2 tablespoons	2 tablespoons
Cornflour	1 teaspoon	1 teaspoon
Cold water	4 tablespoons	4 tablespoons

Shell and de-vein prawns, leaving tails on Soak mushrooms 30 minutes in hot water, discard stems and slice mushrooms finely. Cook noodles in lightly salted boiling water. Rinse in cold water and drain. Bring stock to the boil, add cabbage and noodles and stir in sesame oil. Turn off heat and leave while cooking prawns.

Heat peanut oil in a wok, gently fry garlic and ginger for a few seconds, add prawns and toss on high heat, stirring constantly for 2-3 minutes or until they change colour. Add mushrooms and toss.

Combine soy, cornflour, water to a smooth liquid and add to pan. Stir until it boils and thickens, about 1 minute. Ladle the hot soup into bowls, put a portion of prawns on top of each serving of soup and serve immediately.

seafood

The Chinese have a way with all kinds of food, but perhaps their most outstanding talent is with seafood. The popularity of crisp prawn cutlets and succulent crabs in black bean sauce in any Chinese restaurant speaks for itself. The secret is in short cooking. Prawns are fried just until they are cooked through. They are never allowed to overcook and toughen. Crabs are quick fried, then married with a sauce which complements their own superb flavour. Fish is steamed with ginger or shallots, or fried just enough to crisp the skin and leave it moist within. Scallops are stir-fried for a few brief minutes with vegetables as delicate in flavour as the scallops themselves. Abalone, sliced paper thin, is cooked only a few minutes from the raw state, served cold or just heated through if canned.

The flavours combined with fish and shell fish give them a special quality. For instance, ginger is used with fish to remove excess fishiness or "sarng" as the Chinese call it. Sesame oil, soy sauce, oyster sauce, sweet sour sauce and black bean sauce all bring out the best in the bounty of the ocean and make seafood cooked the Chinese way truly memorable.

Prawn balls with bamboo shoots

Serves: 6

Ingredients	Metric	Imperial
Raw prawns	500 g	1 lb
Fresh root ginger, finely grated	½ teaspoon	½ teaspoon
Salt	½ teaspoon	½ teaspoon
Soft white bread, crumbed	1 slice	1 slice
Egg yolk	1	1
Cornflour	1 teaspoon	1 teaspoon
Braised bamboo shoots (one large can)	approx. 400g can	1 x 14 oz can
Stock from prawns	250 ml	1 cup
Soy sauce	1 tablespoon	1 tablespoon
Oyster sauce	1 tablespoon	1 tablespoon
Cornflour	2 teaspoons	2 teaspoons
Cold water	1 tablespoon	1 tablespoon

Shell and de-vein prawns and chop finely. Combine in a bowl with ginger, salt, breadcrumbs, egg yolk and 1 teaspoon cornflour. With oiled hands form into small balls. Bring about 500 ml (2 cups) water to the boil in a medium saucepan, put in prawn balls and simmer gently for 10 minutes. Keep warm.

In another pan heat the contents of can of bamboo shoots with 125 ml (½ cup) of the prawn stock mixed with the soy and oyster sauce. Stir in 2 teaspoons cornflour mixed with water and allow to boil and thicken. Combine with the prawn balls drained from the stock, and serve with rice or noodles.

Stir-fried prawns and mustard cabbage

Serves: 3-4

Ingredients	Metric	Imperial
Large raw prawns	250 g	8 oz
Chinese mustard cabbage	1	1
Peanut oil	2 tablespoons	2 tablespoons
Garlic, crushed	1 clove	1 clove
Fresh root ginger, finely grated	½ teaspoon	½ teaspoon
Water	3 tablespoons	3 tablespoons
Soy sauce	1 tablespoon	1 tablespoon
Five-spice powder	¼ teaspoon	¼ teaspoon
Sherry or Chinese wine	1 tablespoon	1 tablespoon
Salt	½ teaspoon	½ teaspoon
Cornflour	1½ teaspoons	1½ teaspoons
Cold water	1 tablespoon	1 tablespoon

Shell and de-vein prawns. Cut mustard cabbage into bite sized pieces, using the thick stems and only the tender part of the leaves.

Heat oil in a wok and add garlic, ginger and mustard cabbage and fry for 2 minutes over high heat, stirring constantly. Add prawns and fry for another minute. Lower heat to medium, add water mixed with sauce, wine and seasonings, cover and simmer for 5 minutes. Add cornflour mixed smoothly with cold water and stir until sauce boils and thickens, about 1 minute. Serve at once with rice or noodles.

Note: If buying frozen prawns which are already shelled, 125 g (4 oz) will be sufficient.

Prawns and mushrooms in black bean sauce

Serves: 4-5

Ingredients	Metric	Imperial
Raw prawns	500 g	1 lb
Dried Chinese mushrooms	6 large	6 large
Canned salted black beans	1 tablespoon	1 tablespoon
Chinese wine or dry sherry	2 tablespoons	2 tablespoons
Garlic, crushed	1 clove	1 clove
Fresh root ginger, finely grated	½ teaspoon	½ teaspoon
Sugar	1 teaspoon	1 teaspoon
Peanut oil	1 teaspoon	1 teaspoon
Sesame oil	2 teaspoons	2 teaspoons
Cornflour	2 teaspoons	2 teaspoons
Water	2 tablespoons	2 tablespoons

Shell and de-vein prawns. Soak mushrooms in hot water for 30 minutes, cut away and discard stems, slice mushrooms finely. Put black beans into a small sieve and rinse under cold tap for a few seconds, drain and mash with a fork. It is easiest to do this on a wooden board. Put mashed beans into a bowl and mix with wine, garlic, ginger and sugar.

Heat peanut and sesame oils in a wok, add prawns and mushroom slices and stir-fry for 1 minute. Add bean mixture, lower heat, cover and simmer for 5 minutes. Add cornflour mixed smoothly with water, return to boil and stir until thickened. Serve immediately with rice or noodles.

Fried prawn balls with snow peas

Serves: 4-6

Ingredients	Metric	Imperial
One quantity prawn balls (see page 24) with 1 clove crushed garlic added.		
Peanut oil for deep frying		
Snow peas, strings removed	250 g	8 oz
Fish or chicken stock	250 ml	1 cup
Cornflour	2 teaspoons	2 teaspoons
Cold water	1 tablespoon	1 tablespoon
Oyster sauce	1 tablespoon	1 tablespoon
Sugar	½ teaspoon	½ teaspoon

Make prawn balls as described on page 24. Lightly grease hands with sesame oil and form into small balls about 2.5 cm (1-inch) in diameter. (You may use peanut oil if sesame oil is not available, but sesame oil does give a delightful flavour to the prawns.)

Heat oil in a wok or small deep frying pan and, when hot, put in about 4 or 5 of the balls at a time. Fry, turning with a perforated spoon, for 3 minutes or until golden. Lift out of oil and drain on absorbent paper. Keep warm.

When all the prawn balls are fried, pour off all but 1 tablespoon of the oil in the wok, and on high heat, toss the snow peas in the oil until they turn bright green. This takes about 1½ minutes. Push peas to side of pan, pour in stock, add cornflour mixed with water and cook, stirring, until clear and thickened, about 1 minute. Stir in oyster sauce and sugar. Stir snow peas into the sauce.

Arrange prawn balls on a dish, spoon snow peas and sauce over and serve immediately.

NOTE: This dish cannot be made with cooked prawns. But if snow peas are not available, substitute sliced broccoli, sliced celery, or sliced Chinese mustard cabbage for the snow peas.

Stir-fried Prawns and Mustard Cabbage (See page 34)

Scallops with snow peas

This delicate dish must not be overcooked so have seasonings measured and cornflour mixed with water in readiness for adding to pan. And serve straight away.

Serves: 2-3

Ingredients	Metric	Imperial
Scallops	250 g	8 oz
Leeks	2	2
Snow peas	125 g	4 oz
Peanut oil	2 tablespoons	2 tablespoons
Fresh root ginger, finely grated	½ teaspoon	½ teaspoon
Cornflour	2 teaspoons	2 teaspoons
Water	60 ml	¼ cup
Soy sauce	1 teaspoon	1 teaspoon
Salt	½ teaspoon	½ teaspoon

Wash scallops and drain well. Wash leeks thoroughly, making sure to get rid of all sand and grit. Cut white part of leeks into thin diagonal slices. Remove strings from snow peas.

Heat oil in wok or frying pan and fry the leeks and ginger for a minute over medium heat. Add scallops and fry on high heat, stirring, for 1 minute. Add snow peas and toss with other ingredients for just 1 minute longer. Push to side of pan, add cornflour mixed with water and soy sauce and stir until thickened, about 1 minute. Stir in scallops and vegetables, sprinkle with salt and serve immediately.

Note: If leeks are not available substitute white part of 10 shallots, cut into 2.5 cm (1-inch) pieces.

Fried crab in black bean sauce

Perhaps the most favoured shellfish preparation in Chinese restaurants. To be enjoyed to the fullest the crab should be picked up in the fingers and eaten. That is the only way to make sure all of the delicious, sweet flesh is prised from the shell.

Serves: 4

Ingredients	Metric	Imperial
Fresh crabs	1 medium	1 medium
Canned salted black beans	1 tablespoon	1 tablespoon
Garlic, crushed	1 large clove	1 large clove
Soy sauce	1 tablespoon	1 tablespoon
Sugar	1 teaspoon	1 teaspoon
Peanut oil	4 tablespoons	4 tablespoons
Garlic, cut in two	1 clove	1 clove
Fresh root ginger	2 slices	2 slices
Hot water	8 tablespoons	8 tablespoons
Cornflour	2 teaspoons	2 teaspoons
Cold water	1 tablespoon	1 tablespoon
Shallots, chopped	3	3
Egg, slightly beaten	1	1

Wash crab well, scrubbing away any mossy patches on the shell. Remove hard top shell and fibrous tissue or "dead men's fingers" and also discard stomach bag attached to shell below the eyes. With a heavy cleaver chop body of crab into 4 or 6 pieces, leaving legs attached. Separate large claws from body and crack shell of claws so sauce can penetrate.

Rinse the black beans in a strainer under cold water for a few seconds, then drain. Mash beans well and mix with the crushed clove of garlic. Mix with the soy sauce and sugar.

Heat oil in a wok or large frying pan and fry halved clove of garlic and slices of ginger until they start to brown, then remove from pan. Over high heat fry the pieces of crab, stirring and turning them constantly for 4 or 5 minutes or until shells are bright red. Remove crab pieces from pan. Add black bean mixture to the oil and fry for 1 minute, then add hot water and crab pieces, stir well, cover pan and cook for 3 minutes. Stir in the cornflour mixed with cold water, stir until sauce boils and thickens, then add shallots and egg and stir until egg sets. Serve at once with steamed white rice to soak up the salty sauce.

Abalone in oyster sauce

Serves: 4-5

Ingredients	Metric	Imperial
Abalone	1 x approx. 460 g can	1 x 16 oz can
Chinese dried mushrooms	4	4
Snow peas or	12	12
Chinese mustard cabbage	4 leaves	4 leaves
Shallots	4	4
Sauce:		
Oyster sauce	1 tablespoon	1 tablespoon
Soy sauce	1 teaspoon	1 teaspoon
Chinese wine or brandy	1 tablespoon	1 tablespoon
Water	185 ml	¾ cup
Cornflour	2 teaspoons	2 teaspoons

Drain liquid from can of abalone. Slice abalone in paper thin slices. Soak mushrooms in hot water for 30 minutes, then cut off and discard stalks and slice each mushroom into 4. String snow peas or cut mustard cabbage into bite sized pieces. Cut shallots into similar lengths.

Sauce: Combine all liquid ingredients, add a little to the cornflour and mix until smooth, then combine with remaining liquid. Bring to the boil in a small pan, stirring constantly. Add mushrooms, peas or cabbage and shallots. Cook, stirring, until the vegetables are tender but still crisp — about 2 or 3 minutes. Add abalone and just heat through. Do not cook abalone on high heat or for longer than is necessary to just heat it or it will toughen.

Whole fried snapper
with mushrooms

Serves: 5-6

Ingredients	Metric	Imperial
Snapper, whole	1.5 kg	3 lb
Salt and pepper	to taste	to taste
Cornflour for coating		
Braized mushrooms (see page 90)		
Shallots	6	6
Fresh root ginger, finely grated	½ teaspoon	½ teaspoon
Peanut oil	1 tablespoon	1 tablespoon
Cornflour	3 teaspoons	3 teaspoons
Fish stock or water	¾ cup	¾ cup
Oyster sauce	1 tablespoon	1 tablespoon
Soy sauce	1 teaspoon	1 teaspoon
Peanut oil for deep frying		

Buy fish cleaned and scaled but complete with head and tail.
Wash fish well, and dry inside and out with paper towels. With
sharp knife slash flesh diagonally 3 or 4 times on each side.
Rub over with salt and a little pepper, then dip in cornflour
to coat all over. Dust off excess cornflour. Set aside while
preparing sauce.

Cut half the braized mushrooms into thin slices and reserve
remaining whole mushrooms for garnish. Chop shallots, not too
finely. Heat oil and gently fry shallots and ginger for 1 minute,
then stir in fish stock and the cornflour mixed with a little cold
water. Stir until sauce boils and thickens. Add mushrooms and
heat through, then remove from heat and add oyster sauce and
soy sauce. Cover and keep in a warm place while frying fish.

Heat oil in a wok or frying pan and when smoking hot put in
the fish and spoon oil over the parts that are not immersed. Turn
once after 4 or 5 minutes. The fish should be cooked through
in approximately 12 minutes. Lift out of the oil, drain for a
minute on absorbent paper, then place on a dish and pour the
sauce over. Garnish with the reserved whole mushrooms and if
liked, a few shallot curls. Serve at once.

Fish with crab sauce

Serves: 5-6

Ingredients	Metric	Imperial
Fillets of bream	1 kg	2 lb
Fresh root ginger, finely grated	½ teaspoon	½ teaspoon
Salt	1 teaspoon	1 teaspoon
Cornflour	2 teaspoons	2 teaspoons
Oil for deep frying		

Sauce:

Peanut oil	2 tablespoons	2 tablespoons
Shallots, chopped	6	6
Fresh root ginger, finely grated	½ teaspoon	½ teaspoon
Chicken or fish stock	8 tablespoons	8 tablespoons
Crab meat	180 g	6 oz
Pepper	pinch	pinch
Cornflour	2½ teaspoons	2½ teaspoons
Cold water	1 tablespoon	1 tablespoon

With a sharp knife, remove skin from fish. To do this sprinkle a little salt on the end of the fillet near the tail to enable it to be grasped without slipping. Then slide a knife between the skin and flesh, working towards the head of the fish. Wash fish and pat dry. Lay the fillets on a chopping board and rub with the grated ginger. Cut fillets into halves lengthways, then into bite sized pieces. Toss in a mixture of salt and cornflour.

Heat peanut oil in a small deep pan or wok and quickly fry the fish, not too many pieces at a time, for 1 minute over medium heat. Drain on absorbent paper and keep warm while preparing sauce.

Sauce: Heat oil and gently fry shallots and ginger for a few seconds, stirring, then add stock, cover and simmer for 3-4 minutes. Add crab meat, heat through for not longer than a minute. Season with pepper. Mix cornflour smoothly with the cold water and stir into sauce. Continue stirring over medium heat until sauce boils and thickens. Taste and add salt if necessary. Arrange fish pieces on a dish, spoon sauce over and serve at once.

Crisp skin fish with sweet sour sauce

Serves: 3-4

Ingredients	Metric	Imperial
Whole snapper	750 g	1½ lb
Salt	1 teaspoon	1 teaspoon
Five-spice powder	½ teaspoon	½ teaspoon
Cornflour	¼ cup	¼ cup
Egg, beaten	1	1
Sweet sour sauce:		
Carrot	1	1
Frozen peas	2 tablespoons	2 tablespoons
Onion	1 small	1 small
Soy sauce	1 tablespoon	1 tablespoon
Chinese wine or dry sherry	1 tablespoon	1 tablespoon
Tomato sauce	3 tablespoons	3 tablespoons
Vinegar	2 tablespoons	2 tablespoons
Sugar	2 tablespoons	2 tablespoons
Water	185 ml	¾ cup
Cornflour	1 tablespoon	1 tablespoon
Cold water	2 tablespoons	2 tablespoons
Peanut oil	2 tablespoons	2 tablespoons
Garlic, crushed	1 clove	1 clove
Fresh root ginger, finely grated	¼ teaspoon	¼ teaspoon
Preserved melon shreds, optional	2 tablespoons	2 tablespoons

Have fish cleaned and scaled, but with head and tail left on. Wash well and wipe dry with paper towels. Slash flesh of fish diagonally on both sides and then slash in opposite direction to form diamond shapes. Mix salt and five-spice powder together and rub well into all surfaces of the fish, including slashes. Now prepare sauce.

Sweet Sour Sauce: Peel carrot and cut into thin slices. Bring to the boil in a little lightly salted water and add the peas. Boil for 2 minutes, drain and drop into cold water to set colour. Peel the onion, cut into quarters lengthways, then cut each quarter across into two. Separate layers of onion.

Combine soy sauce, wine, tomato sauce, vinegar, sugar and water and stir until sugar dissolves. Mix cornflour smoothly with the cold water. Heat oil, add garlic, ginger and prepared vegetables and fry for 2 minutes. Add combined sauce mixture, bring to the boil, then stir in cornflour and cook, stirring until thickened. Remove from heat and stir in melon shreds. Keep warm while frying fish.

To fry fish: Put oil to heat in a wok or frying pan and while it is heating, dip fish into beaten egg and then into the cornflour, making sure all surfaces are coated. When oil is smoking hot, dust off excess cornflour and lower the fish gently into the wok. With a ladle pour oil over the side of the fish that is uppermost. Fry for 4 minutes, turn fish and continue frying and spooning oil over. Fish should be cooked through in 8-10 minutes. Drain on absorbent paper, place on dish and serve at once, accompanied by a bowl of the sweet sour sauce.

Fried fish with vegetables

Serves: 3-4

Ingredients	Metric	Imperial
Celery	3 stalks	3 stalks
Chinese dried mushrooms	6	6
Onions	2 small	2 small
Carrots	2 small	2 small
Fish fillets	500 g	1 lb
Cornflour	3 teaspoons	3 teaspoons
Salt	½ teaspoon	½ teaspoon
Five-spice powder	½ teaspoon	½ teaspoon
Egg	1	1
Plain flour for coating		
Peanut oil for deep frying		

Sauce:

Peanut oil	1 tablespoon	1 tablespoon
Fresh root ginger, finely grated	1 teaspoon	1 teaspoon
Shallots, chopped	2	2
Oyster sauce	2 tablespoons	2 tablespoons
Soy sauce	1 teaspoon	1 teaspoon
Chinese wine or dry sherry	1 tablespoon	1 tablespoon
Cornflour	2 teaspoons	2 teaspoons
Water	125 ml	½ cup

Prepare vegetables first and set aside. Slice celery finely in diagonal slices. Soak mushrooms in hot water for 30 minutes or until soft, discard stems and cut in thin slices. Cut onions in quarters lengthways, then cut each quarter in half. Separate onion layers. Slice carrots into very thin circles, put into a small saucepan or wok with just enough cold water to cover, bring to the boil and boil for 1 minute. Drain.

Cut fish in bite sized pieces and dust with the combined cornflour, salt and five-spice powder. Dip in beaten egg, then in plain flour. Deep fry a few pieces at a time in hot oil until crisp and golden, drain on absorbent paper and keep hot.

Sauce: Heat 1 tablespoon peanut oil in wok, add the ginger and shallot and stir for 1 minute. Add the vegetables and toss over high heat for 2 minutes. Move vegetables to side of wok and pour all remaining sauce ingredients in centre, having mixed the cornflour smoothly with the water. Stir over medium heat until it boils and thickens, then stir in the vegetables. Place fish on serving plate, pour sauce with vegetables over and serve at once.

Fried prawns with ginger

Serves: 3-4

Ingredients	Metric	Imperial
Large raw prawns	500 g	1 lb
Fresh root ginger, finely grated	1 teaspoon	1 teaspoon
Cornflour	3 teaspoons	3 teaspoons
Salt	1 teaspoon	1 teaspoon
Peanut oil for deep frying		
Lemon wedges for serving		

Shell and de-vein prawns, wash and drain well or blot water with absorbent kitchen paper Rub ginger well into prawns. Sprinkle cornflour and salt over and mix again.

Heat oil in a wok or frying pan and when very hot, drop in a few prawns at a time. Fry quickly until they change colour, then lift out with a slotted spoon or Chinese wire strainer, drain on absorbent paper and serve hot with wedges of lemon. Each batch of prawns will need to be fried only 2-3 minutes. Do not overcook or they will be tough and dry.

Steamed fish with mushroom sauce

Serves: 3-4

Ingredients	Metric	Imperial
Mushroom sauce:		
Chinese dried mushrooms	8	8
Peanut oil	2 tablespoons	2 tablespoons
Shallots, chopped	4	4
Fresh root ginger, finely grated	½ teaspoon	½ teaspoon
Soy sauce	1 tablespoon	1 tablespoon
Fish stock	185 ml	¾ cup
Cornflour	3 teaspoons	3 teaspoons
Cold water	1 tablespoon	1 tablespoon
Snapper or jewfish fillets	750 g	1½ lb
Salt and pepper	to taste	to taste
Fresh root ginger, finely	½ teaspoon	½ teaspoon
Shallots	6	6

Mushroom sauce: Soak mushrooms in hot water for 30 minutes. Remove and discard stems, slice mushrooms finely. (If you have any leftover braized mushrooms use these instead for extra flavour.) Heat oil and fry shallots and ginger for a few seconds. Then add soy sauce and fish stock mixed together. Bring to the boil, stir in cornflour mixed with cold water and stir until clear and thickened. Keep sauce warm while preparing fish.

Wash and dry fish fillets. Remove skin. Season with salt and very little pepper and rub all over with the ginger. Put fillets on a plate rubbed with a little sesame oil, top with trimmed shallots and steam over boiling water for 8-10 minutes. Pour sauce over fish and serve.

poultry & eggs

Duck is first favourite in Chinese cuisine. It may be roasted, braised, simmered in soy sauce, steamed, dried or salted and every part of it is used including the liver, gizzard, feet and intestines, which are usually sold separately. The carcass of the duck, after choice parts have been eaten, is simmered for stock or congee.

One of China's classic dishes is Peking Duck. The duck is seasoned, brushed over with soy sauce and honey and hung up to dry, then the skin is inflated (a tricky business) and the duck roasted. Only the skin is served for this dish, crackly crisp and fragrant with seasonings. The classic accompaniments are Mandarin Pancakes (page 121) shallot brushes and red bean sauce. The flesh is served separately. This is a task for professional Chinese chefs but Barbecue Style Roast Duck (see page 61) sliced thinly, flesh and skin together, and served with the same accompaniments, makes a good stand-in for Peking Duck.

Chicken cooked Chinese style is a revelation in how to put flavour into the rather tasteless flesh of the mass produced, artificially reared birds that have, in Western countries, taken the place of the farmyard fowl. Try Red Cooked Chicken, simmered in soy sauce with special flavourings added. Or Chicken in Black Bean Sauce. Even simple fried chicken can be given a lift by serving it with a small dish of salt mixed with five-spice powder for sprinkling over.

All kinds of eggs are used by the Chinese, but since duck, goose, quail or plover eggs may be rather difficult to come by, the recipes here are based on hen eggs. A word about those ''thousand year eggs'' you've probably heard of and perhaps wondered about. There's a bit of poetic license in the naming of them. They are duck eggs which are coated with a mixture of limy clay, ashes and salt to preserve them, then buried for approximately 100 days. When they are shelled it is found that they are firm and jellied and have undergone a chemical change which has coloured them black outside and vivid green in the yolk. They are served and eaten raw, usually as a cold hors d'oeuvre, dipped in a mixture of soy sauce and finely grated fresh root ginger.

Much more popular are the little round omelettes called eggs foo yong; or egg rolls filled with pork or prawn and served as hors d'oeuvrès or in soup, or a fantastic, crab-filled omelette. And these are the recipes I have included in this chapter.

Egg roll

Serves: 8 as part of a selection of hors d'oeuvres

Ingredients	Metric	Imperial
Eggs	5	5
Salt	½ teaspoon	½ teaspoon
Pepper	small pinch	small pinch
Peanut oil	1 tablespoon	1 tablespoon
Sesame oil	1 teaspoon	1 teaspoon
Filling:		
Minced lean pork	185 g	6 oz
Salt	½ teaspoon	½ teaspoon
Soy sauce	1 tablespoon	1 tablespoon
Sesame oil	¼ teaspoon	¼ teaspoon
Cornflour	1 teaspoon	1 teaspoon
Finely chopped Chinese parsley	1 teaspoon	1 teaspoon
Shallots, finely chopped	2	2

Beat eggs well and add salt and pepper. Reserve a tablespoon of the beaten egg for sealing the egg rolls. Heat a small omelette pan and grease entire base of pan lightly with a little of the peanut oil and sesame oil mixed together. Pour about 2-3 tablespoons of the egg mixture into pan and make a thin omelette cooking it on one side only. Turn onto a plate. Repeat with more oil and more of the egg mixture. There should be 4 or 5 omelettes, depending on the size of your pan. Divide filling into the same number of portions as there are omelettes.

Place each omelette on a board, cooked side up, and spread filling almost to the edge, using an oiled spatula or back of an oiled tablespoon. Roll up like a Swiss roll and seal edges of omelette with reserved beaten egg. Place on a plate lightly oiled with the same oil used for cooking the omelette.

Put plate in a steamer or on a rack in a saucepan of boiling water, cover and steam for 15 minutes. (The plate should be a little smaller than the steamer or pan to allow steam to circulate.) Remove from heat, cool slightly, then cut into diagonal slices and serve hot or cold as an hors d'oeuvre.

Filling:
Put pork, salt, soy sauce and sesame oil into container of electric blender and blend until almost a paste. Since the mixture is thick it will be necessary to switch blender on and off frequently, and move mixture onto the blades with a spatula. Turn into a bowl and mix in the other ingredients, combining well.

Egg roll with prawn filling

Serves: 8 as part of a selection of hors d'oeuvres

Ingredients	Metric	Imperial
Filling:		
Raw prawns, shelled	185 g	6 oz
Monosodium glutamate, optional	pinch	pinch
Salt	1 teaspoon	1 teaspoon
Sesame oil	1 teaspoon	1 teaspoon
Cornflour	1 teaspoon	1 teaspoon
Shallots, finely chopped	1 tablespoon	1 tablespoon

Make omelettes as in previous recipe.

Filling: Chop prawns very finely and mix in other ingredients, proceed as above.

Crab omelette

My father was not what you would call a domesticated man —
but he could make a crab omelette that was unlike any other
crab omelette I ever tasted. I don't know whether it stemmed
from his own inventiveness or whether the recipe was given
him by one of his good friends, a Chinese dentist-turned-
restaurateur who discovered there was more money to be made
filling people's stomachs than filling their teeth.

Dad would go to the market and choose himself the biggest,
heaviest, freshest crab he could find and bring it home, still
alive and bent on escape. I seem to remember that at this point
he did a quick fade out, leaving the crab to the none-too-tender
ministrations of our cook. But when it had been steamed to
flavoursome succulence and the meat carefully extracted from
shell and claws, Dad took over once more and combined eggs,
crab, shallots into a culinary masterpiece. He never did write
down his recipe, but I have managed to reconstruct something
very like it.

Serves: 2-4

Ingredients	Metric	Imperial
Eggs	4	4
Salt and pepper		
Crab meat	250 ml	1 cup
Lemon juice	squeeze	squeeze
Peanut oil	2 teaspoons	2 teaspoons
Sesame oil	1 teaspoon	1 teaspoon
Shallots, finely chopped	3	3
Green chilli, finely chopped	1	1

Beat eggs slightly, as for a French omelette. Season with
½ teaspoon salt and ¼ teaspoon freshly ground black pepper.
Season crab meat with salt and pepper to taste and a squeeze
of lemon juice. Heat both kinds of oil in a large, heavy omelette
pan and gently fry the shallots and chilli for a minute or two.
Pour in the beaten eggs and cook until set and golden on the
bottom, creamy on top. Meanwhile heat crab meat in a separate
pan. Spoon crab meat down the centre of the omelette and
fold over once. Slide on to a plate and serve hot.

Eggs foo yong with sprouts

Serves: 6

Ingredients	Metric	Imperial
Eggs	6	6
Salt	1 teaspoon	1 teaspoon
Fresh bean sprouts	2 cups	2 cups
Shallots, finely chopped	6	6
Oil	for frying	for frying

Beat eggs with salt. Wash and drain sprouts well, removing any brown "tails" or loose skins. Add sprouts and shallots to beaten egg. Heat peanut oil in a heavy frying pan, or 1 teaspoon oil in a wok. Pour in 125 ml (½ cup) of the egg mixture. Cook until brown on underside, turn and cook other side. Repeat with remaining mixture. Serve with a sweet-sour sauce (see page 123).

Eggs Foo Yong with Prawns
Follow recipe above but omit bean sprouts and add about 250 ml (1 cup) cooked prawns, shelled, de-veined and roughly chopped.

Eggs Foo Yong with Meat
Omit bean sprouts and add 250 ml (1 cup) finely chopped cooked pork, beef or chicken.

Red cooked chicken

"Red cooking" is the term applied to cooking in soy sauce. The liquid that remains after cooking is called a "master sauce" and may be frozen for future use. Cook chicken drumsticks this way for taking on picnics or serving at buffet parties. Fragrant with ginger and anise, red cooked chicken will surely become one of your favourites.

Serves: 8-10 as part of a large menu; 4-5 as a main meal with rice.

Ingredients	Metric	Imperial
Chicken, whole	1.75 kg	3½ lb
Cold water	375 ml	1½ cups
Soy sauce	375 ml	1½ cups
Chinese wine or dry sherry	60 ml	¼ cup
Fresh root ginger, peeled and sliced	5 cm piece	2 inch piece
Garlic	1 clove	1 clove
Star anise	10 sections	10 sections
Sugar	1½ tablespoons	1½ tablespoons
Sesame oil	2 teaspoons	2 teaspoons

Wash chicken well and leave to drain while preparing other ingredients. Choose a saucepan into which the chicken will just fit so that the soy liquid covers as much of the bird as possible. Put chicken into saucepan, breast down, then add all the ingredients except sesame oil. Bring slowly to the boil, then lower heat, cover and simmer very gently for 15 minutes. With tongs, turn chicken over, replace lid and simmer 20 minutes, basting breast with soy mixture every 5 minutes.

Remove from heat, leave covered in the saucepan until cool. Lift chicken out of sauce, place on serving platter and brush with sesame oil. This gives the chicken a glistening appearance as well as extra flavour.

Traditionally the chicken is placed on a chopping board and cut in two lengthways with a sharp cleaver. Each half is chopped into 3.5 cm (1½-inch) strips and reassembled in the original shape. If this proves too much of an undertaking simply carve the chicken into joints. Serve at room temperature with some of the cooking liquid as a dipping sauce.

Marbled Tea Eggs (See page 113)

Oven roasted spiced chicken

This method of preparation is particularly suitable for chicken drumsticks, thighs or wings. If it is not possible to buy selected joints, a whole chicken may be used. See variation.

Serves: 6-8
Oven temperature: 170-190ºC (350-375ºF)
Cooking time: 45 minutes to 1 hour

Ingredients	Metric	Imperial
Chicken pieces	1.5 kg	3 lb
Soy sauce	90 ml	1/3 cup
Peanut oil	60 ml	¼ cup
Chinese wine or dry sherry	1 tablespoon	1 tablespoon
Garlic	1 clove	1 clove
Salt	½ teaspoon	½ teaspoon
Finely grated fresh root ginger	½ teaspoon	½ teaspoon
Five-spice powder	2 teaspoons	2 teaspoons

Wash chicken pieces, dry well on paper towels. In a large shallow dish mix together the soy sauce, oil and wine. Crush garlic to a pulp with salt and add to soy mixture together with ginger and five-spice. Mix well. Place chicken joints in marinade and turn to coat all sides. Cover and marinate for 1 hour or more.

Remove chicken from the marinade, place in a roasting pan in one layer and spoon about 2 tablespoons of the marinade over. Roast in a moderate oven for 45 minutes to 1 hour or until chicken is brown and crisp, basting every 20 minutes with the marinade. Serve hot or cold.

Wings need about 45 minutes roasting time, drumsticks from 45-55 minutes and thighs 1 hour. Thighs should be roasted skin side uppermost.

Variation:
Make a marinade as above and rub it well all over a 3½ lb roasting chicken. Spoon some of the marinade into the cavity of the chicken as well. Marinate for 1 hour, then roast as above, turning the chicken first on one side and then on the other so it is browned all over. Baste frequently. Finish cooking chicken breast upwards. It should take about 1 hour 45 minutes. To serve, carve chicken as for Red Cooked Chicken (see page 54).

Chicken and Walnuts with Straw Mushrooms (See page 58)

Chicken and almonds with straw mushrooms

Serves: 4

Ingredients	Metric	Imperial
Whole chicken breasts	2	2
Cornflour	3 teaspoons	3 teaspoons
Salt	1 teaspoon	1 teaspoon
Five-spice powder	½ teaspoon	½ teaspoon
Shallots	6	6
Straw mushrooms	1 x approx. 430 g can	1 x 15 oz. can
Canned bamboo shoot	1	1
Oil	for deep frying	for deep frying
Blanched almonds	1 cup	1 cup
Stock	125 ml	½ cup
Light soy sauce	1 teaspoon	1 teaspoon
Extra cornflour	1 teaspoon	1 teaspoon
Cold water	1 tablespoon	1 tablespoon

Remove skin from chicken breasts and with a sharp knife cut flesh from bones. (Skin and bones may be simmered in a little water and used for stock.) Cut chicken meat into small dice. Combine cornflour, salt and five-spice powder and sprinkle over chicken. Toss to coat. Cut shallots into bite sized lengths. Drain straw mushrooms and cut each mushroom in half. Dice bamboo shoot.

Heat oil and deep fry almonds until golden. Drain and set aside. Fry chicken pieces, a few at a time, in deep oil over high heat just until they change colour. This takes about 1 minute for each lot. As they are fried, lift them out with a slotted spoon and drain on absorbent paper.

Pour off all but 2 tablespoons oil. Add vegetables to pan and stir-fry over high heat for 1 minute. Add stock. Mix soy and extra cornflour with cold water, add to pan, allow to boil and thicken. Add chicken pieces and heat through. Turn off heat, stir in almonds and serve at once with rice or noodles.

Note: Peeled walnuts may be used instead of almonds.

Chicken in black bean sauce

Serves: 2-3

Ingredients	Metric	Imperial
Chicken breast	1 large	1 large
Bean sprouts or	125 g	4 oz
Celery	3 stalks	3 stalks
Canned salted black beans	2 teaspoons	2 teaspoons
Soy sauce	1 teaspoon	1 teaspoon
Garlic, crushed	1 clove	1 clove
Sherry	1 tablespoon	1 tablespoon
Cornflour	2 teaspoons	2 teaspoons
Cold water	½ cup	½ cup
Oil	1 tablespoon	1 tablespoon

Cut chicken meat off the bone. Save bone for stock. Dice the meat into even sized pieces. Wash and pick over the bean sprouts and leave to drain. Cut celery in thin diagonal slices. Put the black beans in a bowl and mash with a fork. Combine with soy sauce, garlic, sherry and half the water. Mix the cornflour into the remaining water.

Heat oil in a wok, add the black bean mixture and stir until it boils. Add chicken and cook, stirring, for 2 minutes. Add cornflour and stir constantly until it boils and thickens, about 1 minute. Add the bean sprouts and toss in the sauce for 1 minute longer. Serve at once.

Braised chicken and mushrooms with Chinese parsley

Boiled rice or noodles should be served with this dish to take up the large quantity of delicious sauce.

Serves: 4-6

Ingredients	Metric	Imperial
Chinese dried mushrooms	12	12
Dried wood fungus, optional	2 tablespoons	2 tablespoons
Chicken breasts or	1 kg	2 lb
roasting chicken	1.25 kg	2½ lb
Sesame oil	1 tablespoon	1 tablespoon
Peanut oil	1 tablespoon	1 tablespoon
Light soy sauce	1 tablespoon	1 tablespoon
Cornflour	2 tablespoons	2 tablespoons
Garlic	2 cloves	2 cloves
Salt	½ teaspoon	½ teaspoon
Canned salted yellow beans	2 tablespoons	2 tablespoons
Extra peanut oil for frying	2 tablespoons	2 tablespoons
Chopped Chinese parsley	125 ml	½ cup
Chicken stock	250 ml	1 cup
Chinese wine or dry sherry	2 tablespoons	2 tablespoons

Soak mushrooms in hot water 30 minutes. Soak fungus 10 minutes. Discard stems of mushrooms. If mushrooms are large, cut in halves or quarters. Cut chicken breasts into halves, then with a heavy cleaver chop each half through the bone into 3 or 4 pieces. If using a whole chicken, cut into small pieces. Mix together the sesame oil, peanut oil and soy sauce and pour over the chicken. Add 1 tablespoon of the cornflour and mix well.

Crush garlic with salt. Put beans into a strainer and rinse under cold water for a few seconds. Drain well, then mash with a fork and mix with the garlic.

Heat oil in wok and stir-fry the chicken for about 3 minutes on high heat until colour changes. Move chicken to side of wok and put bean mixture in centre. Fry for 1 minute, then mix in the chicken. Add half the Chinese parsley, the stock and wine. Cover and simmer for 5-7 minutes. Mix remaining cornflour with a tablespoon of cold water, stir in and keep stirring until sauce boils and thickens. Serve at once sprinkled with remaining coriander.

Barbecue style roast duck

Serves: 4
Oven temperature: 170-190°C (350-375°F)
Cooking time: 1¾ hours

Ingredients	Metric	Imperial
Roasting duck	1.75 kg	3½ lb
Garlic, crushed	1 clove	1 clove
Finely grated fresh root ginger	1 teaspoon	1 teaspoon
Hoi sin sauce	1 teaspoon	1 teaspoon
Sesame paste	1 teaspoon	1 teaspoon
Wheat corn paste or honey	1 tablespoon	1 tablespoon
Soy sauce	1 tablespoon	1 tablespoon
Salt	1 teaspoon	1 teaspoon
Pepper	½ teaspoon	½ teaspoon

Wash duck inside and out, remove neck and giblets and reserve for making stock. Combine all other ingredients in a small saucepan and heat gently until syrup or honey melts and all are smoothly incorporated. Simmer for 2 minutes, adding a spoonful of water if it seems too thick.

Rub marinade all over duck, inside and out. Reserve remaining marinade to serve as a sauce with the duck. Put duck into oven bag or wrap in foil. If using oven bag, follow manutacturer's instructions and do not fail to make 3 or 4 holes in top of bag near the tie.

Turn duck breast side downwards in roasting pan and cook in a moderate oven for 45 minutes. Turn duck breast side up and cook a further 45 minutes to 1 hour. Remove from bag, carve duck and serve hot with reserved marinade, Mandarin pancakes, shallots and plum or red bean sauce.

Braised duck with lily buds and mushrooms

Serves: 3-4
Cooking time: approximately 35-40 minutes

Ingredients	Metric	Imperial
Roasting duck	1.5 kg	3 lb
Chinese dried mushrooms	8	8
Dried lily buds (golden needles)	20	20
Finely grated fresh root ginger	1 teaspoon	1 teaspoon
Pepper	¼ teaspoon	¼ teaspoon
Salt	½ teaspoon	½ teaspoon
Hoi sin sauce	1 teaspoon	1 teaspoon
Soy sauce	2 teaspoons	2 teaspoons
Peanut oil	2 tablespoons	2 tablespoons
Stock	125 ml	½ cup
Cornflour	1 teaspoon	1 teaspoon
Cold water	1 tablespoon	1 tablespoon

Remove giblets and neck from inside duck and keep for making stock. With a heavy cleaver split duck in half lengthways. Wash and dry well with absorbent paper.

Combine ginger, salt, pepper, hoi sin sauce and 1 teaspoon of the soy sauce. Rub well all over duck. Soak mushrooms and lily buds in hot water for 20 minutes. Cut off mushroom stems and discard. Squeeze excess water from caps. Cut lily buds in halves crossways. (It is quicker if you lay them in a neat bundle and cut them all at once.)

Heat oil in a wok or heavy frying pan. With a knife scrape as much marinade as possible off duck and reserve. Brown duck on both sides. (If using a flat frying pan a little more oil will be necessary, but after browning duck pour off all but 2 tablespoons.) Add mushrooms and lily buds and fry for a minute or two longer. Add 185 ml (¾ cup) of the water mushrooms have soaked in, mixed with the reserved marinade. Cover pan, lower heat and simmer 15 minutes. Turn duck over, simmer 20 minutes longer or until duck is tender. Turn off heat. Place duck on board and with a sharp chopper separate wing, leg and thigh. Chop remaining pieces into 3.5 cm (1½ inch) slices. Arrange on dish with mushrooms and lily buds.

Spoon off as much fat as possible from pan, then add stock and remaining soy sauce. Bring to the boil. Stir in cornflour mixed smoothly with cold water and continue stirring until sauce boils and thickens. Pour over duck and serve immediately with boiled rice.

Braised duck with green peas and cashew nuts

Serves: 3-4

Ingredients	Metric	Imperial
Roasting duck	1.25 kg	2½ lb
Salt	1½ teaspoons	1½ teaspoons
Five-spice powder	½ teaspoon	½ teaspoon
Peanut oil	4 tablespoons	4 tablespoons
Raw cashews	1 cup	1 cup
Hot stock	250 ml	1 cup
Soy sauce	1 tablespoon	1 tablespoon
Finely grated fresh root ginger	½ teaspoon	½ teaspoon
Garlic, crushed	1 clove	1 clove
Peas, fresh or frozen	1 cup	1 cup
Cornflour	1½ teaspoons	1½ teaspoons

If duck is frozen, thaw completely. Use neck and giblets to make stock (see page 16). Cut duck into serving pieces and rub well all over with mixture of salt and five-spice powder.

Heat oil in a wok and fry cashews over medium heat until crisp and golden. Remove nuts and set aside on absorbent paper. Add duck to wok and brown well over high heat. Add stock, soy sauce, ginger and garlic. Lower heat, cover and simmer 35-40 minutes or until duck is tender. Add peas after 20 minutes. Mix cornflour smoothly with cold water, stir into gravy until it boils and thickens. Add cashews, mix and serve at once with rice or noodles.

Roast duck, Szechwanese style

Serves: 4-5
Oven temperature: 170-190°C (350-375°F)
Cooking time: 2 hours, 20 minutes

Ingredients	Metric	Imperial
Roasting duck	3 kg	5 lb
Salt	3 teaspoons	3 teaspoons
Black peppercorns	2 teaspoons	2 teaspoons
Chinese parsley (Coriander) optional	1 whole plant	1 whole plant
Finely grated fresh root ginger	1½ teaspoons	1½ teaspoons
Shallots, chopped	4	4
Five-spice powder	½ teaspoon	½ teaspoon
Honey	1 tablespoon	1 tablespoon
Chinese wine or dry sherry	1 tablespoon	1 tablespoon
Sesame oil	2 teaspoons	2 teaspoons
Soy sauce	1 tablespoon	1 tablespoon
Red food colouring	½ teaspoon	½ teaspoon

Remove neck and giblets of duck from body cavity, wash duck inside and out and dry thoroughly with absorbent kitchen paper. Pick off any pin feathers or quills that remain.
Roast the whole black peppercorns in a dry pan for a few minutes, then crack coarsely with a rolling pin. Wash and dry fresh Chinese parsley (coriander), chop leaves and stem. Reserve the well-washed root. Combine all seasonings and the red colouring and rub well inside and outside duck. Put any coarse leaves of shallot and the coriander root inside the bird. Cover with plastic wrap or foil and refrigerate overnight, or at least 4 hours.
Preheat oven to moderate. Half-fill a roasting pan with hot water and place a rack in the pan. The water should not reach the rack. Put duck on rack, breast upwards, and roast in a moderate oven for 30 minutes. Cover with foil and continue cooking for another 30 minutes. Lower heat to slow, 150-160°C (300-325°F) turn duck breast downwards, place foil over duck and roast for a further 30 minutes. Turn duck breast upwards again and continue cooking for 30 minutes, then remove foil to allow duck to brown for 15-20 minutes. Carve duck and serve with Mandarin pancakes, plum sauce and pieces of shallot.

pork & beef

Pork is the most popular meat in China. Until recent times beef was seldom available for food as cattle were scarce and, in any case, were considered far too valuable as working animals.

Any cut of pork or beef may be used for dishes requiring long cooking. But for the quick, stir-fried dishes so prominent in Chinese cuisine the best cuts are beef fillet, rump or Scotch fillet and pork fillet or chump. These cuts are not cheap but in Chinese cooking a pound of meat will comfortably serve six, because it is combined with vegetables which predominate in quantity, has a well-seasoned sauce and is eaten with rice or noodles. You couldn't stretch a pound of meat six ways in a Western meal, but as part of a Chinese meal with perhaps a soup and a vegetable dish, it is satisfying and very much in keeping with today's health conscious thinking on nutrition.

Meat is always cut in very thin slices or shreds so it can cook quickly, and each piece should be small enough not to require further cutting at the table, since knives are not part of the table setting. If the meat is partially frozen it is firmer to handle and easier to slice paper thin.

Cheaper cuts of lean meat such as round or blade steak may be used for stir-fried dishes if they are tenderised first. This is the Chinese method. Shred or slice meat as directed. For a pound of meat dissolve ½ teaspoon bicarbonate of soda in 3 table-spoons water. Add to meat with salt and other seasonings and knead well until meat absorbs liquid. Refrigerate for 2 hours or longer, overnight if possible. Proceed with the recipe in the usual way. This method is used in many Chinese restaurants, making cheaper cuts of meat as tender as the choicest fillet.

Fillet of beef in black bean sauce

Substitute another suitable vegetable (see note on page 71) when broccoli is out of season, or prepare this dish without vegetables.

Serves: 4

Ingredients	Metric	Imperial
Fillet or Scotch fillet	500 g	1 lb
Canned salted black beans	1½ tablespoons	1½ tablespoons
Garlic, crushed	2 cloves	2 cloves
Soy sauce	1 tablespoon	1 tablespoon
Water	8 tablespoons	8 tablespoons
Sugar	1½ teaspoons	1½ teaspoons
Cornflour	2 teaspoons	2 teaspoons
Broccoli, sliced	125 g	4 oz
Peanut oil	2 tablespoons	2 tablespoons
Sesame oil	1 teaspoon	1 teaspoon

Cut beef in very thin slices and then into shreds, discarding any fat. Put black beans into a small strainer and rinse under cold tap for a few seconds. Drain, then mash with a fork. Combine beans with soy sauce, water, and sugar. Mix cornflour with a tablespoon of the liquid. Peel broccoli stems and slice very finely Divide flower heads into small sprigs. Bring lightly salted water to the boil in a small saucepan, drop in broccoli and return to boil. Boil for just 1 minute. Drain and rinse with cold water Set aside.

Heat oils in a large wok and over high heat fry the beef, tossing and stirring constantly until colour changes. Add garlic, and toss for a few seconds, then add bean mixture. Bring to boil, then lower heat, cover and simmer for 5 minutes. Add cornflour and stir until thickened, then add broccoli and stir until heated through, about 1 minute. Serve immediately with rice.

Red cooked beef

Cold meat Chinese style is an experience in subtle blending of flavours. Cooked in a master sauce, cooled and sliced paper thin, it makes a silk purse out of the sow's ear known as gravy beef!

Serves: 10-12 as part of a Chinese meal.

Ingredients	Metric	Imperial
Shin of beef in one piece	1.5 kg	3 lb
Cold water	750 ml	3 cups
Soy sauce	375 ml	1½ cups
Chinese wine or dry sherry	60 ml	¼ cup
Fresh root ginger, peeled and sliced	5 cm piece	2-inch piece
Garlic, peeled	2 whole cloves	2 whole cloves
Whole star anise	2	2
Sugar	2 tablespoons	2 tablespoons
Sesame oil	1 tablespoon	1 tablespoon

Put beef in a saucepan just large enough to hold it. Add all other ingredients, bring to the boil, then turn heat low so that it simmers very gently. Cover and simmer for 3 hours or until beef is very tender. Test by piercing with a skewer — it should be able to penetrate easily. Turn beef once or twice so that all of it is immersed in the liquid at some time during cooking. Uncover pan and cook for a further 15 minutes, pouring sauce over the beef with a ladle every 5 minutes. Let the beef cool in the sauce, turning it over after an hour. Chill until serving time, then place on a board and with a sharp Chinese chopper, cut into very thin slices. Arrange on a dish.

Note: Save the master sauce, as the cooking liquid is now called, and freeze it for future use. A spoonful added to a dish in place of stock will give a rich, delicious flavour. If whole star anise is difficult to obtain, use about 16 of the broken sections.

Shredded five-spice beef with broccoli

Serves: 4-5

Ingredients	Metric	Imperial
Beef fillet or rump	500 g	1 lb
Garlic, crushed	1 clove	1 clove
Salt	1 teaspoon	1 teaspoon
Fresh ginger, grated	½ teaspoon	½ teaspoon
Cornflour	2 teaspoons	2 teaspoons
Five-spice powder	½ teaspoon	½ teaspoon
Broccoli	250 g	½ lb
Cornflour	1 teaspoon	1 teaspoon
Water	2 tablespoons	2 tablespoons
Soy sauce	1 tablespoon	1 tablespoon
Peanut oil	3 tablespoons	3 tablespoons
Sesame oil	2 teaspoons	2 teaspoons

Cut beef into very thin slices, then cut slices into fine shreds. Remove any fat. Crush the garlic with the salt and rub garlic and ginger into beef, mixing thoroughly. Mix 2 teaspoons cornflour and the five-spice powder together and sprinkle over beef. Toss to distribute evenly. Slice broccoli thinly, or divide into small sprigs. Mix together the cornflour, water and soy sauce.

Heat oils in a wok and when hot add the beef and fry, over high heat, stirring constantly, for 2 minutes or until meat changes colour. Add broccoli and fry for 3 minutes, stirring and tossing ingredients together all the time. Add cornflour mixture and stir until it boils and thickens, then stir well to coat beef and broccoli with sauce. Serve immediately with boiled rice or noodles.

Shredded beef with bean sprouts and walnuts

Serves: 5-6

Ingredients	Metric	Imperial
Beef, fillet or rump	500 g	1 lb
Garlic, crushed	1 clove	1 clove
Salt	½ teaspoon	½ teaspoon
Fresh root ginger, finely grated	½ teaspoon	½ teaspoon
Soy sauce	1 tablespoon	1 tablespoon
Hoi sin sauce	1 teaspoon	1 teaspoon
Onion	1 large	1 large
Green capsicum	½	½
Fresh bean sprouts	250 g	8 oz
Bamboo shoot, canned	1	1
Cornflour	2 teaspoons	2 teaspoons
Cold water	2 tablespoons	2 tablespoons
Oil	4 tablespoons	4 tablespoons
Canned salted walnuts	½ cup	½ cup

Cut beef into very thin shreds. Crush garlic with salt, combine with ginger, hoi sin sauce and soy sauce. Cut onion into half lengthways, then into very thin lengthways slices. Dice capsicum. Wash and drain bean sprouts. Cut bamboo shoot into thin slices, then into squares. Mix cornflour and cold water and set aside.

Heat 2 tablespoons oil in a wok and fry onion and green pepper quickly, stirring all the time, until onion is soft and slightly coloured, about 3-4 minutes. Remove from pan. Heat remaining 2 tablespoons oil and fry beef on high heat, stirring and tossing constantly, until all the beef has lost its red colour and is turning brown. Add bean sprouts and bamboo shoot and toss until heated through, about 2 minutes. Move beef mixture to side of pan, add cornflour mixture to pan and stir until it boils and thickens. Return onions and capsicum to pan. Turn off heat, add walnuts and mix all well together. Serve on a bed of boiled noodles or rice.

Stir-fried beef and vegetables in oyster sauce

Serves: 4

Ingredients	Metric	Imperial
Fillet or rump steak	500 g	1 lb
Soy sauce	2 tablespoons	2 tablespoons
Salt	½ teaspoon	½ teaspoon
Chinese wine or dry sherry	1 tablespoon	1 tablespoon
Monosodium glutamate	¼ teaspoon	¼ teaspoon
Mixed vegetables (see note below)	500 g	1 lb
Peanut oil	3 tablespoons	3 tablespoons
Garlic, finely chopped	1 large clove	1 large clove
Fresh root ginger, finely grated	½ teaspoon	½ teaspoon
Stock or water	125 ml	½ cup
Cornflour	3 teaspoons	3 teaspoons
Cold water	2 tablespoons	2 tablespoons
Oyster sauce	2 tablespoons	2 tablespoons
Shallots	4	4

Slice meat very, very thinly against the grain and cut into shreds approximately 3.5 cm (1½-inches) long. Combine soy sauce, wine, salt, monosodium glutamate and mix well with the beef. Let it stand while preparing the vegetables.

Use any combination of vegetables and cut them into pieces of the same size as the beef. Heat 1 tablespoon of the oil in a wok, add ginger and garlic, stir for 3 or 4 seconds, then add all the vegetables and stir constantly over high heat for 2½-3 minutes. Remove from heat and turn into a bowl, together with any liquid in wok.

Heat wok again, add remaining 2 tablespoons oil and when very hot put in the beef and stir-fry over high heat about 2 minutes or until colour changes. Add stock and bring to the boil, then add cornflour mixed smoothly with the cold water and return to the boil, stirring constantly. Cook until liquid thickens, about 1 minute. Stir in oyster sauce, return fried vegetables and toss well together. Add shallots, and serve immediately with boiled rice.

Note: Vegetables in stir-fried dishes. Use a combination of Chinese mustard cabbage, other types of Chinese cabbage, snow peas, green or red capsicum, cucumber slices, beans, broccoli, onion, cauliflower or carrot. If using beans, cauliflower or broccoli it is necessary to blanch them in boiling water for just 2 minutes before frying. Slice beans thinly into diagonal slices, slice cauliflower or broccoli finely or divide into small sprigs. Other vegetables may be fried from the raw state.

Fried beef and long beans

Serves: 3-4

Ingredients	Metric	Imperial
Long beans	12-15	12-15
Scotch fillet or rump steak	375 g	12 oz
Garlic, crushed	1 clove	1 clove
Fresh root ginger, finely grated	½ teaspoon	½ teaspoon
Salt	½ teaspoon	½ teaspoon
Five-spice powder	½ teaspoon	½ teaspoon
Cornflour	2 teaspoons	2 teaspoons
Cold water	1 tablespoon	1 tablespoon
Oyster sauce	2 tablespoons	2 tablespoons
Soy sauce	1 tablespoon	1 tablespoon
Peanut oil	2 tablespoons	2 tablespoons
Stock	125 ml	½ cup

Wash and cut beans into 5 cm (2-inch) lengths. Shred beef finely and mix well with the garlic, ginger, salt and five-spice. Mix cornflour smoothly with water, stir in oyster sauce and soy sauce.

Heat oil in a wok or heavy frying pan, add beef and beans and stir-fry over high heat for 2 minutes. Add stock and allow to boil up, then stir in cornflour and sauce mixture and stir constantly until it boils and thickens. Toss the beef and beans in the sauce and serve at once with rice.

Beef with lotus root

Serves: 3-4

Ingredients	Metric	Imperial
Fillet or rump steak	250 g	8 oz
Soy sauce	1 tablespoon	1 tablespoon
Salt	½ teaspoon	½ teaspoon
Garlic, crushed	1 clove	1 clove
Fresh root ginger, finely grated	½ teaspoon	½ teaspoon
Five-spice powder	¼ teaspoon	¼ teaspoon
Peanut oil	2 tablespoons	2 tablespoons
Stock or water	125 ml	½ cup
Cornflour	1 tablespoon	1 tablespoon
Cold water	2 tablespoons	2 tablespoons
Lotus root, canned	12 slices	12 slices

Cut meat into paper thin slices, sprinkle soy sauce, salt, garlic, ginger and five-spice powder over, and mix well with the hand to season all the pieces of beef.

Heat oil in a wok or large frying pan and when very hot add the beef and toss over high heat until colour changes. Add stock, stir in cornflour mixed with cold water and boil, stirring, until gravy becomes thick and clear. Add sliced lotus root and heat through. Serve with boiled rice.

Braised pork with noodles

Serves: 4-5

Ingredients	Metric	Imperial
Dried mushrooms	6	6
Dried wood fungus	1 tablespoon	1 tablespoon
Belly pork	500 g	1 lb
Soy sauce	1½ tablespoons	1½ tablespoons
Brandy or Chinese wine	1 tablespoon	1 tablespoon
Cornflour	2 tablespoons	2 tablespoons
Peanut oil	2 tablespoons	2 tablespoons
Garlic, crushed	2 cloves	2 cloves
Hot water	500 ml	2 cups
Mustard cabbage or white cabbage	250 g	8 oz
Oyster sauce	2 tablespoons	2 tablespoons
Egg noodles	250 g	8 oz
Oil, extra	2 tablespoons	2 tablespoons

Soak mushrooms and fungus in hot water for 30 minutes. Remove rind from pork or ask butcher to remove pork rind. Cut in slices as narrow as possible. Cut slices into pieces about 2.5 cm (1-inch) square. Combine soy sauce, wine and cornflour and mix well with pork. Heat 2 tablespoons peanut oil in a wok, add garlic, then turn in pork and fry for a few minutes, stirring. Add mushrooms and fungus, sliced, and the hot water. Cover and simmer 35 minutes or until pork is tender.

Meanwhile, cook the noodles in lightly salted boiling water until just tender. Drain in a colander and run cold water over to remove excess starch and stop cooking. Drain well. Heat extra oil in another pan and fry the noodles, first on one side, then on the other. Add cabbage to the pork and cook for 1 minute longer. Serve pork on a bed of hot noodles.

Crisp fried pork with
sweet sour sauce

Pork may be fried once and set aside with ingredients for sauce prepared beforehand. At serving time make the sauce and fry pork briefly once more.

Serves: 4-6

Ingredients	Metric	Imperial
Pork fillet or pork chops	500 g	1 lb
Soy sauce	1 tablespoon	1 tablespoon
Chinese wine or dry sherry	1 tablespoon	1 tablespoon
Salt	½ teaspoon	½ teaspoon
Pepper	¼ teaspoon	¼ teaspoon
Five-spice powder	¼ teaspoon	¼ teaspoon
Plain flour	250 ml	1 cup
Warm water	185 ml	¾ cup
Peanut oil	1 tablespoon	1 tablespoon
Egg white	1	1
Extra peanut oil	for deep frying	for deep frying

Sweet sour sauce:

	Metric	Imperial
Light soy sauce	1 tablespoon	1 tablespoon
Chinese wine or dry sherry, optional	1 tablespoon	1 tablespoon
Tomato sauce	3 tablespoons	3 tablespoons
White vinegar	2 tablespoons	2 tablespoons
Sugar	2 tablespoons	2 tablespoons
Water	185 ml	¾ cup
Cornflour	1 tablespoon	1 tablespoon
Onion	1 small	1 small
Water chestnuts, sliced	½ cup	½ cup
Red capsicum, diced	1	1
Frozen or fresh green peas	3 tablespoons	3 tablespoons
Peanut oil	2 tablespoons	2 tablespoons
Garlic, crushed	1 clove	1 clove
Fresh root ginger, finely grated	¼ teaspoon	¼ teaspoon
Preserved melon shreds, optional	2 tablespoons	2 tablespoons

If using pork chops, remove rind. Cut pork into 1 cm (½-inch) slices, then into 2.5 cm (1-inch) squares. Mix with the soy sauce, wine, salt, pepper and five-spice powder. Refrigerate while preparing batter.

Mix flour and warm water to a smooth batter with a wooden spoon, stir in oil, allow to stand for 30 minutes. Beat egg white until stiff and fold in.

Heat oil. Dip pieces of pork in batter and deep fry a few at a time over medium heat until pork is cooked and batter golden. Drain on absorbent paper and set aside. Make sauce.

Sweet Sour Sauce: Combine soy sauce, wine, tomato sauce, vinegar, sugar and water in a bowl and stir until sugar dissolves.

Mix cornflour smoothly with about 1 tablespoon of cold water. Peel onion, cut into four lengthways, then cut each quarter across into two. Separate layers of onion. Heat oil, add garlic, ginger and all the vegetables and fry for 2 minutes. Add combined sauce mixture, bring to the boil, then stir in cornflour and cook, stirring constantly until thickened. Remove from heat and stir in melon shreds.

Shortly before serving reheat oil and once more fry pork, a few pieces at a time, on high heat for just a few seconds. This second frying makes the batter very crisp. Drain on absorbent paper and when all the pork is fried arrange on a plate, pour hot sauce over and serve immediately.

Barbecued pork spareribs

Serves: 6-8
Cooking time: approximately 1 hour
Oven temperature: 200-230°C (400-450°F) reduced to 170-190°C (350-375°F)

Ingredients	Metric	Imperial
Pork spareribs	1.5 kg	3 lb
Garlic, crushed	2 large cloves	2 large cloves
Salt	1 teaspoon	1 teaspoon
Fresh root ginger, finely grated	1 teaspoon	1 teaspoon
Soy sauce	2 tablespoons	2 tablespoons
Red bean paste or hoi sin sauce	1 tablespoon	1 tablespoon
Sesame sauce	2 teaspoons	2 teaspoons
Honey	1 tablespoon	1 tablespoon
Sherry	1 tablespoon	1 tablespoon
Peanut oil (add only if using fillet)	1 tablespoon	1 tablespoon

Ask butcher to cut rack of bones into lengths of about 4 or 5 bones each. At home, use a sharp knife to cut between the bones but do not separate them.

Combine garlic, crushed with salt, and all other ingredients in a bowl and beat well with a spoon to mix together. The sesame sauce should be stirred well in the jar before measuring the required amount as the oil floats on top and the paste settles at the bottom. Pour marinade over the pork and rub on all sides and between the bones. Marinate for an hour or more.

Half fill a roasting pan with water and place a rack in the pan or across the top. Water should not touch rack. Place the marinated pork on the rack and cook in a hot oven for 20 minutes, then reduce heat to moderate, turn pork and cook a further 25 minutes. Pork may require further cooking. When barbecued pork is ready it should be reddish brown all over, touched with dark brown here and there, as if barbecued over open coals. Cooking time may be anything between 45 minutes and 1 hour, depending on thickness of pork.

Barbecued Pork

Serves: 4-6
Cooking time: approximately 45 minutes
Oven temperature: 200-230°C (400-450°F)

Ingredients	Metric	Imperial
Pork belly or fillet	500 g	1 lb
Garlic	3 cloves	3 cloves
Finely grated ginger	½ teaspoon	½ teaspoon
Salt	1 teaspoon	1 teaspoon
Soy sauce	1 tablespoon	1 tablespoon
Honey	1 tablespoon	1 tablespoon
Chinese wine or sherry	1 tablespoon	1 tablespoon
Five-spice powder	½ teaspoon	½ teaspoon

With a sharp knife remove rind from pork, or ask butcher to do
this for you. Cut pork into strips the length of the piece of
pork and about 2.5 cm (1-inch) wide. Crush garlic with salt
and combine with all the other ingredients in a large bowl. Put
in the pork, mix well together so that the pork is covered on all
sides with the barbecue mixture. Allow to marinate for 15
minutes or longer.

Half fill a roasting pan with hot water and place a wire rack
across the top of the pan. Place pork on rack and roast in hot
oven 30 minutes. Turn pork strips over, brush with remaining
marinade and cook further 15 minutes or until well glazed and
lightly touched with dark brown on the spots where the honey
marinade has caramelised. Cut in slices to serve. Serve immediately,
with plum sauce or hoi sin sauce for dipping.

Pork and bamboo shoot in black bean sauce

Serves: 6

Ingredients	Metric	Imperial
Pork belly	750 g	1½ lb
Salt	1 teaspoon	1 teaspoon
Bamboo shoot, canned	1	1
Canned salted black beans	2 tablespoons	2 tablespoons
Chinese wine or sherry	1 tablespoon	1 tablespoon
Soy sauce	1 tablespoon	1 tablespoon
Garlic	2 cloves	2 cloves
Oil	2 tablespoons	2 tablespoons
Hot water	2 cups	2 cups

With a sharp knife remove and discard skin and cut pork into 2.5 cm (1-inch) squares. Sprinkle ½ teaspoon salt over pork, mix well and set aside. Cut bamboo shoot into thin slices, then into pieces about 1 inch across. Rinse beans by placing in a strainer and running cold water through for a few seconds. Drain beans, put on chopping board and mash with a fork. Combine in a bowl with the sherry and soy sauce. Crush garlic with remaining ½ teaspoon salt and add.

Heat oil in a wok and fry the pork on high heat for 3-4 minutes or until brown, stirring all the time. Add bamboo shoot and bean mixture and fry for a few minutes longer. Then add hot water, stir once, cover and simmer 40 minutes. Serve with boiled rice.

Pork with chestnuts

Serves: 4-5

Ingredients	Metric	Imperial
Pork belly	500 g	1 lb
Dried chestnuts	125 g	4 oz
Garlic, crushed	2 cloves	2 cloves
Salt	1 teaspoon	1 teaspoon
Soy sauce	1 tablespoon	1 tablespoon
Chinese wine or brandy	1 tablespoon	1 tablespoon
Peanut oil	2 tablespoons	2 tablespoons
Hot water	625 ml	2½ cups
Cornflour	2 teaspoons	2 teaspoons
Cold water	2 tablespoons	2 tablespoons

With a sharp knife remove skin from pork, or ask butcher to do
this Cut pork into thin slices then into small dice. Mix with
garlic crushed with salt, soy sauce and wine or brandy. Let stand
for 1 hour. Pour boiling water over dried chestnuts in a bowl,
allow to stand for 30 minutes. Pour off water and replace with
more boiling water. Stand for a further 30 minutes. Drain off
water before using.

Heat oil in a wok and fry marinated pork, stirring constantly,
until brown. Add the chestnuts and stir well, then add hot
water, cover and simmer for 35-40 minutes. Mix cornflour with
cold water. Push pork and chestnuts to side of pan and add
cornflour mixture to liquid in pan. (There should be about 1
cup liquid. If not, make up quantity with water.) Cook until
thick, stirring constantly. Garnish, if liked, with pieces of
shallot. Serve with rice.

Pork with abalone, Szechwan style

Hot and spicy, this dish reflects the Indian influence on Chinese food as Szechwan is on the border of China and India.

Serves: 4

Ingredients	Metric	Imperial
Lean pork fillet	250 g	8 oz
Abalone	1 x 500 g can	1 x 16 oz can
Peanut oil	2 tablespoons	2 tablespoons
Fresh root ginger, finely chopped	1 teaspoon	1 teaspoon
Garlic, finely chopped	1 clove	1 clove
Cornflour	2 teaspoons	2 teaspoons
Cold water	1 tablespoon	1 tablespoon
Chilli sauce	1 teaspoon	1 teaspoon

Cut pork fillet into very thin slices. Drain canned abalone, reserving liquid from can. Cut abalone into paper thin slices.

Heat oil in wok with ginger and garlic, add pork and stir-fry over high heat until colour changes. Add liquid from can of abalone, cover and simmer for 10 minutes. Add cornflour mixed with cold water, stir until boiling and thickened, then stir in chilli sauce. Mix well. Add abalone slices and leave only just long enough to heat through, about 1 minute. Abalone must not be overcooked or it will be tough. Serve with boiled rice or noodles.

Braised pork balls and mushrooms

Serves: 4-5

Ingredients	Metric	Imperial
Dried Chinese mushrooms	16-20	16-20
Minced pork	250 g	8 oz
Shallots, finely chopped	4	4
Finely grated fresh ginger	½ teaspoon	½ teaspoon
Salt	1½ teaspoons	1½ teaspoons
Soy sauce	2 tablespoons	2 tablespoons
Sherry or Chinese wine	1 tablespoon	1 tablespoon
Sugar	2 teaspoons	2 teaspoons
Sesame oil	1 teaspoon	1 teaspoon
Cornflour	1½ teaspoons	1½ teaspoons
Cold water	2 teaspoons	2 teaspoons

Wash mushrooms well, then soak in hot water for 30 minutes. While mushrooms soak, prepare pork balls. Combine minced pork, shallots, ginger and salt thoroughly and form into small balls approximately 2.5 cm (1-inch) in diameter. Bring to the boil in a small saucepan just enough water to simmer the balls in. Add them to the boiling water, cover and simmer for 10 minutes.

While they simmer, squeeze excess water from mushrooms and with a sharp knife remove and discard the stems. Mix together the soy sauce, sherry, sugar and sesame oil. When the pork balls have cooked for 10 minutes add the mushrooms and soy sauce mixture, stir well, cover and simmer for 25 minutes.

With a slotted spoon remove pork balls and mushrooms to a plate. There should be about 185 ml (¾ cup) liquid left in the pan. Measure and add water if necessary to make up to this quantity. Return cooking liquid to pan, bring to the boil, then stir in the cornflour mixed with cold water. Cook, stirring, until it thickens, about 1 minute. Then stir in pork and mushrooms, heat through and serve with noodles or rice.

vegetables

One of the great joys of cooking and eating Chinese food is discovering the many exotic, fascinating, flavourful vegetables that are such an important part of the Chinese diet. Visit your city's Chinatown and find them — in cans, dried, or freshly grown by Chinese market gardeners.

Try lotus root — the very name has a poetic sound. The slices with their lacy design have a texture similar to potato; water chestnuts, white and crisp within the brownish black skin; bamboo shoots, ranging from tiny, finger-sized ones (find these in cans of braised bamboo shoots) to large shoots as thick as a man's arm; miniature corn cobs so tender you eat them cob and all.

Browse among the dried ingredients for the Chinese mushrooms that add their distinctive flavour to so many dishes. You cannot substitute fresh mushrooms or dried Continental mushrooms. Chinese mushrooms are expensive, but so light in weight that you get a lot for your money. Then there are dried lily buds or "golden needles" as they are sometimes called. Dried wood fungus is another fascinating ingredient, there are various kinds available, but the one used in these recipes is called "wun yee" or "cloud ear fungus". In its dried state it resembles small, dusty fragments of black paper, but soak them in hot water and watch them swell into smooth shapes of translucent brown. They add no flavour, but provide wonderful, crunchy, resilient texture.

Among the fresh vegetables are crisp white sprouts of green mung beans, sold by the pound in plastic bags; snow peas, tender and sweet, with edible pods; numerous kinds of melon and different varieties of greens. There is delicate Chinese cabbage (wong bok), white stalks edged with leaves like pale green ruched chiffon, closely packed in a neat oval shape. Vivid green mustard cabbage (gai choy), its leaves springing vigorously from a central stalk. The leaf rib is the choicest part, tender and crisp with a distinctive mustardy tang. Chard cabbage (bok choy), silvery stemmed with very deep green leaves. Bunches of soup greens, also called gai choy, and pungent fresh coriander, known as Chinese parsley.

Be adventurous. Try vegetables you haven't tried before. And believe me when I say in this and other chapters that fresh vegetables are cooked for just 2 or 3 minutes, some even less. They should be crisp and green, retaining their fresh flavour and texture. Overcooked vegetables have no place in Chinese cuisine.

Bean curd with crab sauce

Serves: 4

Ingredients	Metric	Imperial
Crab meat, fresh, frozen or canned	125 g	4 oz
Peanut oil	2 tablespoons	2 tablespoons
Shallots, roughly chopped	6	6
Finely grated fresh root ginger	½ teaspoon	½ teaspoon
Chicken or fish stock	8 tablespoons	8 tablespoons
Pepper	small pinch	small pinch
Cornflour	2½ teaspoons	2½ teaspoons
Cold water	1 tablespoon	1 tablespoon
Fresh bean curd	8 squares	8 squares

Drain and flake crab and pick over to remove any bony tissue. Heat the oil in a small pan and gently fry shallots and ginger for a minute or so, stirring, until ginger starts to turn golden and shallots are softened. Add stock, cover and simmer for 3-4 minutes. Add crab meat and heat through. Season with pepper, then stir in cornflour mixed to a smooth cream with water. Stir over medium heat until sauce boils and thickens. Add bean curd, spoon sauce over and heat until just about to come to a boil. Do not overcook. Taste and add salt if necessary, serve at once with rice.

Bean curd braised in oyster sauce

Serves: 3

Ingredients	Metric	Imperial
Peanut oil	1 tablespoon	1 tablespoon
Garlic, crushed	1 small clove	1 small clove
Chinese cabbage or mixed vegetables	250 g	8 oz
Stock	2 tablespoons	2 tablespoons
Oyster sauce	1 tablespoon	1 tablespoon
Soy sauce	1 tablespoon	1 tablespoon
Sherry	1 tablespoon	1 tablespoon
Cornflour	1½ teaspoons	1½ teaspoons
Water	2 tablespoons	2 tablespoons
Fresh bean curd	6 squares	6 squares

Heat oil in a wok and gently fry the garlic for 1 minute. Add vegetables cut in bite size pieces and stir-fry on high heat for 2 minutes. Add stock, cover and simmer for 1 minute longer. Mix together the oyster sauce, soy sauce and sherry. Add to wok, stir and simmer. Add cornflour mixed with cold water, and stir until it boils and thickens. Add squares of bean curd, heat through and serve immediately with boiled rice.

Broccoli, bean sprouts and water chestnuts

Serves: 4

Ingredients	Metric	Imperial
Fresh broccoli	500 g	1 lb
Fresh bean sprouts	250 g	8 oz
Water chestnuts, fresh or canned	18 (1 small can)	18 (1 small can)
Dressing:		
Sesame oil	1 tablespoon	1 tablespoon
Peanut oil	2 tablespoons	2 tablespoons

Light soy sauce	3 tablespoons	3 tablespoons
Sugar	1 teaspoon	1 teaspoon

Separate broccoli into small sprigs, trimming off all but the most tender stems. Bring a small pan of lightly salted water to the boil, drop in broccoli, return to the boil and boil for 1 minute. Drain, then run under cold water to stop cooking and set the colour. Wash bean sprouts in cold water and drain in colander. Slice the canned water chestnuts, or peel and slice fresh ones.

Toss well together with combined dressing ingredients.

Young corn cobs and snow peas with bamboo shoot in red sauce

Serves: 4

Ingredients	Metric	Imperial
Young corn cobs	1 x approx. 440 g can	1 x 15 oz can
Snow peas	250 g	8 oz
Canned bamboo shoot	1	1
Oil	1 tablespoon	1 tablespoon
Garlic, crushed	1 clove	1 clove
Finely grated fresh root ginger	¼ teaspoon	¼ teaspoon
Soy sauce	2 tablespoons	2 tablespoons
Five-spice powder	½ teaspoon	½ teaspoon
Sherry	1 tablespoon	1 tablespoon
Sugar	1 teaspoon	1 teaspoon
Cornflour	2 teaspoons	2 teaspoons
Water	2 tablespoons	2 tablespoons

Drain corn. String snow peas. Cut bamboo shoot into thin slices. Heat oil in wok, add garlic and ginger, then vegetables, and stir-fry for 1 minute. Have ready the soy, five-spice, sherry and sugar mixed together. Add to pan. Mix cornflour with the water and stir in, and serve as soon as it boils and thickens.

Young corn cobs and snow peas with cucumber

Serves: 4

Ingredients	Metric	Imperial
Young corn cobs	1 x approx. 440 g can	1 x 15 oz can
Snow peas	250 g	8 oz
Cucumber	1	1
Peanut oil	1 tablespoon	1 tablespoon
Sesame oil	1 teaspoon	1 teaspoon
Crushed garlic	¼ teaspoon	¼ teaspoon
Finely grated fresh root ginger	¼ teaspoon	¼ teaspoon
Salt	to taste	to taste

Drain liquid from can of corn. Remove stems and strings from snow peas. Peel and cut cucumber into 6 mm (¼-inch) slices. Heat peanut oil in a wok, add sesame oil, garlic and ginger and stir once, then turn in corn and snow peas. Fry stirring, for 1 minute over high heat. Add cucumber slices and cook 2 minutes longer. Serve at once.

Mixed braised vegetables

Use a mixture of Chinese cabbage, mustard cabbage, leeks, cauliflower, shallots, beans, in any combination or proportions. Weigh after trimming and slicing.

Serves: 4-6

Ingredients	Metric	Imperial
Sliced vegetables	750 g	1½ lb
Peanut oil	2 tablespoons	2 tablespoons
Sesame oil	1 teaspoon	1 teaspoon
Garlic, crushed	1 large clove	1 large clove
Grated fresh root ginger	1 teaspoon	1 teaspoon
Hot water or stock	125 ml	½ cup

Oyster sauce	1 tablespoon	1 tablespoon
Light soy sauce	2 teaspoons	2 teaspoons
Salt	½ teaspoon	½ teaspoon
Monosodium glutamate	½ teaspoon	½ teaspoon
Cornflour	2 teaspoons	2 teaspoons
Cold water	1 tablespoon	1 tablespoon

Heat oils in wok with garlic and ginger, add vegetables and fry, stirring, for 2 minutes. Add hot water and sauces, salt and monosodium glutamate mixed together. Cover and simmer for 4 minutes. Push vegetables to side of wok, add cornflour mixed with cold water, stir until thick. Toss vegetables in sauce and serve at once with boiled rice.

Heavenly braised vegetables

Serves: 4

Ingredients	Metric	Imperial
Dried Chinese mushrooms	12	12
Dried wood fungus	3 tablespoons	3 tablespoons
Bamboo shoot	1 small can (238 g)	1 small can (8½ oz)
Young corn cobs	1 small can (425 g)	1 small can (15 oz)
Peanut oil	2 tablespoons	2 tablespoons
Sesame oil	1 tablespoon	1 tablespoon
Soy sauce	2 tablespoons	2 tablespoons
Sugar	1 tablespoon	1 tablespoon
Mushroom liquid	500 ml	2 cups

Soak mushrooms in 3 cups hot water 30 minutes. Remove and discard stems, squeeze out excess moisture from caps. Reserve the mushroom liquid. Soak fungus in water 10 minutes, rinse and drain, then cut each piece in two. Slice bamboo shoots thinly. Drain corn.

Heat oil in a wok and fry the mushrooms until brown, about 5 minutes on high heat, stirring all the time. Add remaining ingredients, mix well, then cover and simmer over low heat for 25-30 minutes. Serve with rice.

Braised mushrooms

Serves: 6-8

Ingredients	Metric	Imperial
Dried Chinese mushrooms	125 g	4 oz
Hot water	1 litre	4 cups
Soy sauce	2 tablespoons	2 tablespoons
Sugar	2 tablespoons	2 tablespoons
Sesame oil	1 tablespoon	1 tablespoon
Monosodium glutamate (optional)	¼ teaspoon	¼ teaspoon
Peanut oil	3 tablespoons	3 tablespoons

Wash mushrooms well in cold water. Place in a bowl and pour hot water over, cover and allow to soak for 30 minutes. With sharp knife, cut stems off and discard. Squeeze as much water as possible from the mushrooms, reserving the liquid. To the reserved liquid, add some of the water in which the mushrooms were soaked, enough to make 375 ml (1½ cups). Add the soy sauce, sugar, sesame oil and monosodium glutamate if used. Stir to dissolve sugar.

Heat peanut oil in a small wok or medium saucepan and fry mushrooms over a high heat, stirring and turning, until the undersides are browned. Add liquid mixture, lower heat, cover and simmer for approximately 30 minutes or until all the liquid is absorbed and the mushrooms take on a shiny appearance. Towards end of cooking time, it is advisable to stir occasionally. Serve hot or cold.

Note: Braised mushrooms keep well in the refrigerator. They may be added to other dishes, either whole or sliced.

Young Corn Cobs and Snow Peas with Cucumber (See page 88)

rice
&noodles

Throughout the East, rice is treated with what amounts to reverence. I remember, as a child, once making the mistake of climbing on to the large wooden chest or "rice box" as it was called, in which the month's supply of rice was stored. And I remember, too, my ayah (native nurse) who almost never rebuked me, telling me sternly to get off and show proper respect for the rice. Even as "breaking bread" denotes eating a meal in Western countries, so does "eating rice" embrace the same meaning in the East. To many millions of people in Asia rice is the staff of life, and in China this is especially true.

The most suitable rice for Chinese cooking is short grain or medium grain white rice. Since a moist, clinging result is desirable, do not wash the rice at all, or if there is a lot of loose starch wash it just once or twice. Even if you are very proud of your ability to cook fluffy rice, when serving Chinese food please cook rice the Chinese way. It should not be sticky or gluey, but each perfectly cooked grain, pearly and well defined, should cling to neighbouring grains, making it much easier to pick up with chopsticks! Short and long grain rice are not interchangeable in recipes. Long grain rice absorbs almost twice as much water.

In Chinese stores you will also find sticky or glutinous rice. This is used for special sweet dishes and is not suitable for serving with the savoury dishes in this book.

There is a bewildering array of packaged dry noodles — wide egg noodles, wide rice noodles, fine egg noodles, fine rice noodles, rice vermicelli, cellophane or bean starch noodles.

A selection of Chinese vegetables
1. Soup greens 2. Shallots 3. Fresh root ginger 4. Fresh bean sprouts 5. Chinese dried mushrooms 6. Chinese cabbage 7. Fuzzy melon 8. Bitter melons 9. Garlic 10. Dried lychees 11. Chard cabbage (bok choy) 12. Dried lotus root 13. Chinese parsley (fresh coriander) 14. Giant white radish

Egg noodles

Perhaps the most popular, egg noodles, are made of wheat flour and are sold in 1 lb packets, each packet consisting of seven or eight bundles. An important point about cooking them is that the bundles of noodles must be soaked in hot water for about 10 minutes first. They don't tell you this in the cooking instructions, yet it does make cooking them so much easier. As the bundles soften the strands separate and the noodles cook more evenly than when they are dropped straight into boiling water.

Rice noodles

There are various kinds of rice noodles. Depending on the type of noodle and thickness of the strands, they have to be soaked in cold water for 30 minutes to 1 hour or longer. Drain, drop into fast boiling water and boil for 6-10 minutes, testing every minute after the first 6 minutes so you will know when they are done. As soon as they are tender drain in a colander and rinse well in cold running water. Drain once more. If well rinsed so that no excess starch remains on the noodles, they may be prepared beforehand, then fried or heated in soup before serving.

Rice vermicelli

Rice vermicelli has very fine strands, does not need soaking and cooks very quickly. Drop into boiling water and cook for 2 or 3 minutes only. Drain well. Serve in soups or with dishes that have a good amount of sauce. Or, if a crisp garnish is required, for example a base for presenting prawn fritters or other hot hors d'oeuvres, use rice vermicelli straight from the packet and fry small amounts at a time in deep hot oil for just a few seconds. It will puff and become white as soon as it is immersed in oil, but make sure the oil is hot enough. Lift out quickly on a slotted spoon or wire strainer, drain on absorbent paper.

Cellophane or bean starch noodles

Also known as transparent noodles, bean threads, silver threads or fenszu. For a crisp garnish fry in the same way as rice vermicelli. For including in soups or braised dishes, soak 20 minutes in hot water, drain, then cook in boiling water 15 minutes or until tender.

Boiled rice

Serves: 4

Ingredients	Metric	Imperial
Short grain rice	2 cups	2 cups
Water	2½ cups	2½ cups

Wash rice in one or two changes of cold water and drain in a colander. Bring water to the boil, add rice and stir once. Return to the boil, then turn heat very low, cover pan tightly and cook without lifting lid for 15 minutes.

Savoury boiled rice

Serves: 4-5

Ingredients	Metric	Imperial
Chinese sausages	2	2
Short grain rice	2 cups	2 cups
Water	2½ cups	2½ cups
Salt	2 teaspoons	2 teaspoons
Cooked pork or chicken	250 g	8 oz
Sliced beans or frozen peas	1 cup	1 cup
Finely grated fresh root ginger	½ teaspoon	½ teaspoon
Soy sauce	1 tablespoon	1 tablespoon
Chinese wine, optional	1 tablespoon	1 tablespoon
Cornflour	2 teaspoons	2 teaspoons
Sesame oil	1 teaspoon	1 teaspoon
Oyster sauce	1 tablespoon	1 tablespoon
Shallots, chopped	8	8

Steam sausages for 10 minutes, cut into thin slices. Wash rice in 3 changes of water. Drain. Bring water and salt to the boil, add rice, and when it returns to the boil, lower heat, cover and cook for 5 minutes. In the meantime, mix together sausages and all remaining ingredients, except shallots. When rice has cooked for 5 minutes, spread mixture over the surface of the rice, replace lid and cook for a further 15 minutes on very low heat. Fork meats through rice and serve hot, garnished with shallots.

Conjee

Conjee is a rice gruel or porridge rather like a thick cream soup. The simplest conjee is just rice simmered in water, the proportions being ½ cup raw rice to 6 cups water. Once it comes to the boil it is simmered on low heat for 2 hours or until a thin porridge-like consistency results. Add salt to taste and serve in bowls with pungent accompaniments such as pickles and salted vegetables.

Conjee is a good way to use up leftover cooked rice, especially the hard crust of rice that sometimes forms at the bottom of the pan. Don't throw it away, just add water or stock, chicken bones or pork bones, or a few dried prawns, a little grated ginger and garlic, and simmer gently for an hour or more. A very savoury dish will be the result. You are also saved the trouble of cleaning out pans with rice sticking to them. Serve conjee in bowls like soup.

Serves: 4-6

Ingredients	Metric	Imperial
Cooked rice	2 cups	2 cups
Chicken stock	5 cups	5 cups
Chicken breast, shredded	1	1
Dried Chinese mushrooms, soaked and sliced	4	4
Chinese cabbage, cut into pieces	125 g	4 oz
Leek, finely sliced	1	1
Shallots, chopped	6	6

Simmer rice in stock for 1½ hours or until very soft. Add chicken and mushrooms and cook 10 minutes longer. Stir in cabbage and cook 2 minutes, then add leeks and shallots. Remove from heat and serve at once.

Simple fried rice

Ingredients	Metric	Imperial
Short grain rice	2 cups	2 cups
Water	2½ cups	2½ cups
Sesame oil	2 teaspoons	2 teaspoons
Eggs, beaten	2	2
Salt	¼ teaspoon	¼ teaspoon
Fat bacon	2 rashers	2 rashers
Peanut oil or lard	1 tablespoon	1 tablespoon
Small prawns, optional	250 g	8 oz
Cooked green peas	125 ml	½ cup
Shallots, chopped	250 ml	1 cup
Soy sauce	2 tablespoons	2 tablespoons

Cook rice in water (see page 95), cool and separate grains. Refrigerate if possible. Or use 4 cups cold leftover rice. Heat sesame oil in a frying pan or wok, add eggs seasoned with salt and quickly stir over heat until scrambled. Remove from pan and set aside.

Wipe out pan with a piece of kitchen paper, add finely chopped bacon and fry until crisp. Remove bacon pieces from pan and set aside with the eggs.

Add peanut oil or lard to bacon drippings in pan and when hot add the rice and fry, stirring and tossing, until rice is golden. Add prawns, peas, shallots, mix well and heat through. Sprinkle soy sauce evenly over rice, return eggs and bacon to pan and stir over high heat for 1 minute longer. Serve hot.

Vegetarian fried rice

Serves: 6

Ingredients	Metric	Imperial
Short grain rice	2 cups	2 cups
Water	2½ cups	2½ cups
Dried Chinese mushrooms	60 g	2 oz
Leeks	2	2
Celery	4 stalks	4 stalks
Green beans	250 g	8 oz
Bean sprouts, optional	125 g	4 oz
Coarsely grated carrots	250 ml	1 cup
Sliced bamboo shoot, optional	250 ml	1 cup
Peanut oil	3 tablespoons	3 tablespoons
Sesame oil	1 tablespoon	1 tablespoon
Fresh ginger, finely grated	1 teaspoon	1 teaspoon
Garlic, finely grated	2 cloves	2 cloves
Chopped shallots	250 ml	1 cup
Mushroom liquid	125 ml	½ cup
Soy sauce	2 tablespoons	2 tablespoons
Salt	to taste	to taste

Cook rice in water the day before required or cook it some hours ahead and allow to cool (see page 95). With the fingers, separate grains and spread out rice so grains dry. Refrigerate.

Soak mushrooms in hot water for 30 minutes, then squeeze out as much liquid as possible and reserve this liquid they soaked in. With a sharp knife cut off and discard stems, and cut mushroom caps into thin slices. Wash leeks very well in cold water, making sure all grit is washed away, then cut into thin slices. Use the white portion and only 5-7 cm (2-3-inches) of the green leaves. String celery and green beans and cut into very thin diagonal slices. Wash and drain bean sprouts and pick off any brown "tails"

Heat peanut oil and sesame oil in a large wok or very large frying pan, add ginger and garlic and fry, stirring well, for 30 seconds. Add mushrooms, leeks, celery, beans and carrots and stir-fry over high heat for 3 minutes. Add bean sprouts and bamboo shoot and fry 1 minute longer. Add rice, toss and fry over high heat until heated through. Add shallots. Mix mushroom liquid and soy sauce together, and sprinkle evenly over the rice. Continue stirring to mix well together and season to taste with salt. Serve hot.

Mixed fried rice

To Vegetarian Fried Rice add 1 pair dried Chinese sausages, steamed for 10 minutes, then cut into paper thin diagonal slices; 1 cup diced cooked chicken or pork; 1 cup small prawns, shelled and de-veined. The amount of vegetables used may be reduced, or one or two vegetables omitted.

Boiled noodles

Allow 1 bundle egg noodles for each person. Soak noodles in hot water for about 10 minutes. The strands will separate and enable the noodles to cook evenly. Meanwhile, bring a large saucepan of water to the boil and add a spoonful of peanut oil. Drain the soaked noodles and drop them into the boiling water. When water returns to the boil, cook fine noodles for 2-3 minutes, wide noodles for 3-4 minutes. Do not overcook. Like properly cooked spaghetti, noodles should be tender but still firm to the bite.

At end of cooking time drain noodles in a large colander, then run cold water through the noodles to rinse off excess starch and cool the noodles so they don't continue to cook in their own heat. Drain thoroughly and serve with stir-fried dishes or use in soups and braised noodle dishes.

Soft fried noodles

Proceed as for boiled noodles. When noodles are well drained, spread them on a large baking tray lined with kitchen paper and allow them to dry in the air for at least 30 minutes. A little peanut oil may be sprinkled over them to prevent sticking.

Heat 2 tablespoons each of peanut oil and sesame oil in a wok or frying pan and when very hot add a handful of noodles. When golden on one side, turn and fry other side. Repeat with remaining noodles. It may be necessary to add more oil to the pan if a large quantity of noodles is being fried, but make sure the fresh oil is very hot before adding noodles.

Serve with beef, pork, poultry or vegetable dishes, or combine with stir-fried ingredients for Chow Mein.

Crisp fried noodles

Rice vermicelli and cellophane noodles may be fried in deep hot oil straight from the packet. Egg-noodles need to be cooked first as for soft-fried noodles. Use a larger amount of peanut oil and deep fry in handfuls until crisp and golden brown. These crisp noodles are used mainly as a garnish.

Combination chow mein

Chow Mein, a popular dish in Western countries, is sometimes made with crisp fried noodles, but the authentic recipe calls for soft-fried noodles combined with other ingredients. A delicious way of using up leftovers. The quantities are only a guide, use what you have on hand.

Serves: 6

Ingredients	Metric	Imperial
Fine egg noodles	6 bundles	6 bundles
Peanut oil	for frying	for frying
Garlic, crushed	1 clove	1 clove
Finely grated fresh root ginger	½ teaspoon	½ teaspoon
Barbecued pork, sliced	1 cup	1 cup
Diced cooked chicken	1 cup	1 cup
Sliced abalone	½ cup	½ cup
Sliced Chinese cabbage or mustard cabbage	1 cup	1 cup
	1 cup	1 cup
Bean sprouts, washed and dried	1 cup	1 cup
Shallots, cut in 5 cm (2-inch) lengths	8	8
Sliced bamboo shoots, optional	½ cup	½ cup
Stock or water	½ cup	½ cup
Soy sauce	2 tablespoons	2 tablespoons
Cornflour	2 teaspoons	2 teaspoons
Cold water	2 tablespoons	2 tablespoons

Cook noodles and soft fry as described on page 100. Heat 2 tablespoons peanut oil in a wok and fry the garlic and ginger for a few seconds. Add pork, chicken and abalone, cabbage, bean sprouts, shallots, and bamboo shoot. Stir-fry for a minute or two until heated through. Push ingredients to side of wok.

Add stock and soy sauce, bring to the boil, then stir in cornflour mixed smoothly with the water. Stir until it boils and thickens, then stir in meat and vegetables. Serve over fried noodles.

Braised noodles with chicken

Serves: 4-5

Ingredients	Metric	Imperial
Wide egg noodles	4 bundles	4 bundles
Chicken, boned	500 g	1 lb
Chinese cabbage or mustard cabbage	3 cups	3 cups
Snow peas	12	12
Soy sauce	1 tablespoon	1 tablespoon
Chinese wine or dry sherry	1 tablespoon	1 tablespoon
Cornflour	1 tablespoon	1 tablespoon
Cold water	2 tablespoons	2 tablespoons
Oyster sauce	1 tablespoon	1 tablespoon
Salt	½ teaspoon	½ teaspoon
Peanut oil	2 tablespoons	2 tablespoons
Garlic, crushed	2 cloves	2 cloves
Finely grated fresh root ginger	1 teaspoon	1 teaspoon
Chicken stock	250 ml	1 cup
Shallots, cut in pieces	5	5

Soak noodles in hot water for 10 minutes. Drain. Bring plenty of water to the boil in a large saucepan, drop in bundles of egg noodles and loosen bundles with chopsticks or a fork as they cook. Boil for 3-4 minutes or until they are cooked but still firm. Do not overcook. Drain in a colander and hold under running cold tap to rinse and stop cooking. Drain.

Cut chicken into small squares and pour the soy sauce and sherry over. Mix and allow to marinate while preparing vegetables. Cut stalks of Chinese cabbage into bite sized pieces. Remove strings from snow peas. Mix cornflour with cold water and oyster sauce and salt, and set aside.

Heat oil in a wok and gently fry garlic and ginger for a few seconds. Add chicken and stir-fry over high heat for 2 minutes or until colour changes. Add cabbage and snow peas and fry, stirring, for 1 minute longer. Add stock, bring to the boil, add cornflour mixture and stir until thick. Add well drained noodles and heat through, tossing to mix evenly.

Noodles with braised beef

Serves: 4

Ingredients	Metric	Imperial
Wide egg noodles	4 bundles	4 bundles
Rump or Scotch fillet steak	500 g	1 lb
Garlic, crushed	1 clove	1 clove
Salt	½ teaspoon	½ teaspoon
Finely grated fresh root ginger	¼ teaspoon	¼ teaspoon
Five-spice powder	¼ teaspoon	¼ teaspoon
Peanut oil	2 tablespoons	2 tablespoons
Master Sauce (see page 67)	250 ml	1 cup
Cornflour	2 teaspoons	2 teaspoons
Cold water	1 tablespoon	1 tablespoon
Shallots	10	10

Soak noodles in hot water for 10 minutes, drain, then drop noodles into a large pan of boiling water and cook for 3 minutes or until just tender. Drain in colander, rinse under cold tap and drain once more.

While noodles are draining, cut beef into paper-thin shreds. Rub garlic crushed with salt, ginger and five-spice powder into beef.

Heat oil in a wok and quickly stir-fry the beef over high heat until it changes colour. Add the Master Sauce and bring to the boil. Add cornflour mixed to a smooth paste with cold water and stir until it boils and thickens. Add noodles and heat through. Stir in shallots cut into bite sized pieces and keep turning and mixing noodles and beef in the sauce for a further minute. Serve at once.

Note: If Master Sauce is not available, substitute ½ cup soy sauce and ½ cup water or stock.

Chicken and abalone chow mein

Serves: 4

Ingredients	Metric	Imperial
Chicken breasts	2	2
Abalone	1 x approx. 460 g can	1 x 16 oz can
Shallots	6	6
Canned salted yellow beans	1 tablespoon	1 tablespoon
Finely grated fresh root ginger	¼ teaspoon	¼ teaspoon
Garlic, crushed	1 clove	1 clove
Light soy sauce	1 tablespoon	1 tablespoon
Cornflour	3 teaspoons	3 teaspoons
Oil	2 tablespoons	2 tablespoons
Fried noodles (recipe page 100)	2 bundles	2 bundles

Remove skin and bones from chicken and cut flesh into bite sized pieces. Drain liquid from can of abalone and reserve. Cut abalone into very thin slices. Wash shallots and cut into bite sized lengths. Put salted yellow beans in a small strainer, rinse under cold tap and drain. Mash beans and combine in a small bowl with ginger, garlic, soy sauce and ¼ cup reserved abalone liquid. Combine remaining liquid (about one cup) with cornflour in a separate bowl.

Heat oil in a wok and pour in mashed bean mixture. Let it boil up for a minute, then add chicken pieces and stir fry over high heat for 2 minutes. Add cornflour mixture and stir over medium heat until it boils and thickens. Add noodles and shallots and simmer further 2 minutes. Stir in abalone just until heated through, about 1 minute. Do not overcook abalone or it will toughen. Serve immediately.

snacks, sauces & sweets

Eastern cities never seem to sleep. At any hour of the day or night you will see vendors at street stalls doing a brisk business in snacks both sweet and savoury, for nibbling between meals is a habit that Eastern races are much addicted to.

This is the chapter I most enjoyed testing recipes for. It brought back memories of my childhood, of buying from Chinese street sellers those irresistible snacks known as 'dim sims'. Some of these are ideal for serving as an appetiser course with a meal, while others are purely for breaking the boredom of those long hours between meals.

These delectable hors d'oeuvre and snacks are quite simple to make and within the capabilities of any keen cook who is willing to try. Just follow the recipes and you will be as thrilled as I am at the results you can achieve using simple ingredients and everyday utensils.

Chinese meals don't, as a rule, feature desserts, but at banquets and on special festive occasions sweets are served, often not at the end of a meal but as a break in a succession of savoury dishes. Most readers will prefer, as I do, to serve a sweet as a fitting finale to a Chinese meal. Almond Jelly, Oriental Fruit Basket or Lychees and Oranges are all suitable. The sweet buns and almond biscuits are more in the category of between-meal treats.

Hot hors d'oeuvres

A platter of crisp-fried titbits — prawn, chicken, bacon and so on — with a choice of sauces for dipping. Beside bowls and chopsticks, provide small individual sauce bowls at each place. All preparation may be done beforehand and the hors d'oeuvres fried and drained. Just before serving, fry the morsels a second time. This is not just for reheating — it enhances the crispness of the batter.

Serves: 6-8

Ingredients	Metric	Imperial
Raw prawns	250 g	8 oz
Salt	to taste	to taste
Chicken breast meat	250 g	8 oz
Five-spice powder	¼ teaspoon	¼ teaspoon
Bacon rashers	4	4
Egg rolls, optional (see page 50))	3	3
Batter:		
Plain flour	1 cup	1 cup
Warm water	185 ml	¾ cup
Peanut oil	1 tablespoon	1 tablespoon
Egg white	1	1
Extra peanut oil	for deep frying	for deep frying

Shell and de-vein prawns and if large, cut each prawn in two lengthways. Season lightly with salt. Cut chicken meat into strips the same size as prawns. Make a mixture of 1 teaspoon salt and the five-spice powder and sprinkle ½ teaspoon of this over the chicken. Remove bacon rind and cut rashers into bite sized pieces.

Make egg rolls and after they are cooked and cooled, cut across into slices about the thickness of a finger.

Batter: Sift flour into a bowl, add warm water and beat with a wooden spoon until smooth. Stir in oil and the remaining salt and five-spice mixture. Allow to stand for 30 minutes to 1 hour. Just before using, stiffly beat egg white and fold into batter.

Heat oil for deep frying. With chopsticks or fork dip pieces of prawn, chicken, bacon and egg roll in batter and drop one at a time into the oil. Fry a few pieces at a time over medium heat until golden. Drain on absorbent paper.

Before serving, heat oil again and fry, over higher heat this time, for just a few seconds. Do not put too many pieces into the pan at once or temperature of oil will be reduced. Drain once more and serve, accompanied by sauces for dipping. Chilli-soy sauce, ginger-soy sauce and sweet-sour sauce are all suitable. See page 122 and 123 for sauces.

Prawn toast

A crisp, tasty appetizer to serve with drinks, as a starter to a meal or during the meal, between courses.

Makes: 12 pieces, serves 4-6

Ingredients	Metric	Imperial
Raw prawns	250 g	8 oz
Beaten egg	1 tablespoon	1 tablespoon
Finely grated fresh root ginger	½ teaspoon	½ teaspoon
Salt	½ teaspoon	½ teaspoon
Oyster sauce	1 tablespoon	1 tablespoon
Chilli sauce, optional	1 teaspoon	1 teaspoon
Chinese wine or dry sherry	2 teaspoons	2 teaspoons
Cornflour	2 teaspoons	2 teaspoons
White bread	6 slices	6 slices
Parsley or Chinese parsley	few sprigs	few sprigs
Peanut oil	for deep frying	for deep frying

Shell and de-vein prawns. If using frozen peeled raw prawns defrost completely, drain off liquid and weigh 125 g (4 oz). Chop prawns very finely and mix with beaten egg, ginger, salt, oyster sauce, chilli sauce, wine and cornflour. Trim crusts off bread slices and cut each slice in half, diagonally.

Spread bread with prawn mixture and press a sprig of parsley on top to garnish. Heat oil and put in a few pieces of bread at a time, prawn side downwards. Fry until bread is golden. Drain on absorbent paper and serve hot.

Butterfly prawns

Serves: 4-6

Ingredients	Metric	Imperial
Large raw prawns	12	12
Soy sauce	2 tablespoons	2 tablespoons
Chinese wine or dry sherry, optional	1 tablespoon	1 tablespoon
Garlic, crushed	1 small clove	1 small clove
Salt	¼ teaspoon	¼ teaspoon
Finely grated fresh root ginger	½ teaspoon	½ teaspoon
Cornflour	½ cup	½ cup
Beaten egg	1 large	1 large
Breadcrumbs	for coating	for coating
Peanut oil	for deep frying	for deep frying

Shell and de-vein prawns, leaving tail on. With a sharp knife slit prawns along curve of back but do not cut right through. Combine soy sauce, wine, garlic crushed with salt, ginger. Marinate prawns in this mixture for 15 minutes.

Dip prawns into cornflour, shake off excess, then dip into the beaten egg and finally into the breadcrumbs. Press gently to flatten prawns and firm on the crumb coating.

Heat oil and fry prawns, 2 or 3 at a time, until golden brown, about 2 minutes. Drain on absorbent paper and serve hot with chilli sauce if desired.

Miniature Scallop Rolls (See page 112)

Pork dumplings

Makes: approximately 20

Ingredients	Metric	Imperial
Dried Chinese mushrooms	4	4
Minced pork	250 g	8 oz
Finely chopped bamboo shoot	2 tablespoons	2 tablespoons
Shallots, finely chopped	4	4
Salt	1½ teaspoons	1½ teaspoons
Soy sauce	1 tablespoon	1 tablespoon
Sesame oil	1 teaspoon	1 teaspoon
Finely grated fresh root ginger	½ teaspoon	½ teaspoon
Kau Che Dough (see pages 114, 115)	1 quantity	1 quantity

Soak mushroom in hot water for 30 minutes. Cut off stems
with a sharp knife and discard. Chop mushroom caps finely.
Combine with all other ingredients except the dough. Form into
small balls with lightly oiled hands.

Bring 750 ml (3 cups) pork or chicken stock or water to the
boil, drop in the pork balls, cover and simmer gently for 15
minutes. Allow to cool in the liquid.

Place each ball on a thinly rolled circle of the dough just
large enough to enclose it. Pinch dough together at the top to
seal, keeping a nice round shape. Put dumplings on squares of
oiled greaseproof paper, place in a steamer, cover and steam
for 10 minutes. Serve hot.

Bean Curd with Crab Sauce (See page 85)

Miniature scallop rolls

Makes approximately 20-24

Ingredients	Metric	Imperial
Scallops	185 g	6 oz
Dried Chinese mushrooms	3	3
Water chestnuts, canned or fresh	6	6
Shallots	2	2
Finely grated fresh root ginger	¼ teaspoon	¼ teaspoon
Salt	½ teaspoon	½ teaspoon
Light soy sauce	1 teaspoon	1 teaspoon
Sesame oil	1 teaspoon	1 teaspoon
Spring roll wrappers	5 or 6	5 or 6
Egg	1	1
Plain flour	1½ tablespoons	1½ tablespoons
Peanut oil	for deep frying	for deep frying

Beard scallops, rinse and drain on absorbent paper, then cut into small pieces. Soak mushrooms in hot water 30 minutes, cut off and discard stems, chop mushrooms finely. Chop water chestnuts roughly, leaving pieces large enough to provide a crunchy texture in the filling. Chop shallots finely. Mix these ingredients with the ginger, salt, soy sauce and sesame oil.

Cut each spring roll wrapper into quarters. On each quarter place a teaspoonful of the filling, near one end. Fold pastry over filling, then fold sides in to enclose filling, and roll over again as for the first fold. Beat egg until frothy, add flour and beat again to a smooth, thick paste. Smear end of spring roll pastry with this paste and press gently to seal.

When all are made, fry in deep oil over medium heat until golden brown all over, about 1½ minutes. Drain on absorbent paper and serve hot.

See page 115 for crab meat filling.

Marbled tea eggs

Serves: 6

Ingredients	Metric	Imperial
Eggs	6	6
Black tea	3 tablespoons	3 tablespoons
Salt	1 tablespoon	1 tablespoon
Star anise	2	2

Place eggs in a saucepan, cover with cold water and bring slowly to the boil, stirring gently. (This helps to centre the yolks.) Simmer gently for 7 minutes. Cool eggs thoroughly under running cold water for 5 minutes. Lightly crack each egg shell by rolling on a hard surface. Shell should be cracked all over, but do not remove.

Bring 1 litre (4 cups) water to the boil, add tea leaves, salt and star anise. Put in the eggs and simmer, covered, about 30 minutes or until shells turn brown. Let eggs stand in covered pan overnight if possible, or at least for 30 minutes. Drain, cool and shell them. The whites of eggs will have a delicate marbled pattern on them. Serve the eggs as a snack or as part of a hors d'oeuvre with sauces for dipping.

Pork spring rolls

Make larger spring rolls for snacks. Use the whole spring roll wrapper and enclose 2 tablespoons of filling made by combining equal parts of finely chopped cooked pork and shredded Chinese cabbage. Season with salt and soy sauce. Bean sprouts and finely chopped shallots may be added. Fold in the same way as Miniature Spring Rolls.

Kau che or gow jee

These steamed savouries with a delicately seasoned prawn filling are a specialty on the menu in some Chinese restaurants. The filling is enclosed in thinly rolled, semi-transparent dough shaped like miniature Cornish pasties.

Makes: about 20

Ingredients	Metric	Imperial
Filling:		
Raw prawns	185 g	6 oz
Chopped ham or bacon fat	2 tablespoons	2 tablespoons
Finely chopped bamboo shoot	2 tablespoons	2 tablespoons
Finely chopped shallots	2	2
Finely grated fresh root ginger	½ teaspoon	½ teaspoon
Cornflour	3 teaspoons	3 teaspoons
Sesame oil	1 teaspoon	1 teaspoon
Salt	1 teaspoon	1 teaspoon
Sugar	1 teaspoon	1 teaspoon
Dough:		
Chinese wheat flour	1 cup	1 cup
Cornflour	3 tablespoons	3 tablespoons
Water	220 ml	7 oz
Lard	1 tablespoon	1 tablespoon
Sesame oil	for brushing	for brushing

Filling: Shell and de-vein prawns and cut into small pieces. Combine with all other ingredients, mixing thoroughly. Set aside while making dough.

Dough: Mix Chinese wheat flour and cornflour together in a bowl. Put water and lard into a small saucepan, bring to the boil, cool while counting 20 seconds, then pour onto the flour. Mix well with chopsticks or the handle of a wooden spoon and as soon as it is cool enough to handle knead to a smooth, pliable dough. Divide into two equal portions and mould each to a cylinder approximately 12.5 cm (5-inches) long and 2.5 cm (1-inch) in diameter. Keep dough wrapped in plastic film to prevent surface drying out.

On a smooth surface (a laminated pastry board is ideal) cut 1 cm (½-inch) slices from one of the rolls of dough and flatten with the lightly greased blade of a wide Chinese chopper or a metal spatula. Then roll out to a thin circle about 10 cm (4-inches) in diameter.

Place a teaspoonful of the filling on the dough and bring edges together. Pinch to seal, at the same time fluting the joined edge as for a decorative pie crust.

When the dough from one roll is used up, brush the kau che lightly with sesame oil, place on squares of oiled greaseproof paper and steam for 12 minutes. Repeat with remaining dough and filling. Serve hot with sauces for dipping if desired.

Variation: Crab meat rolls

Make up the following filling and use to fill miniature spring rolls as in the recipe on page 112.

Makes: 20-24

Ingredients	Metric	Imperial
Crab meat, frozen or canned	185 g	6 oz
Dried Chinese mushrooms	4	4
Shallots	2	2
Finely grated fresh root ginger	¼ teaspoon	¼ teaspoon
Salt	½ teaspoon	½ teaspoon
Chinese wine or dry sherry	1 teaspoon	1 teaspoon
Monosodium glutamate, optional	¼ teaspoon	¼ teaspoon

Flake crab meat, removing bony tissue. Drain off any liquid. Soak mushrooms in hot water for 30 minutes, remove and discard stems and chop mushroom caps finely. Slice shallots very thinly. Mix crab, mushrooms, shallots, ginger, salt, wine and monosodium glutamate together.

Dough for steamed buns

This dough is used with a variety of fillings, both savoury and sweet.

Makes: 6-8 buns

Ingredients	Metric	Imperial
Plain flour	2½ cups	2½ cups
Castor sugar	3 tablespoons	3 tablespoons
Baking powder	3½ teaspoons	3½ teaspoons
Softened lard	2 tablespoons	2 tablespoons
Lukewarm water	approx. 125 ml	approx. ½ cup
White vinegar	½ teaspoon	½ teaspoon

Sift flour and baking powder into a bowl, stir in sugar and rub in lard with fingertips until evenly distributed. Add water and vinegar mixed together and knead to a fairly soft dough. Shape into a smooth ball, cover and rest dough for 30 minutes.

Meanwhile, prepare filling and allow to cool completely. To make buns, divide dough into 6 or 8 portions and mould each to a smooth ball. Roll out on a very lightly floured board to a circle about 10 cm (4-inches) across. Put a heaped teaspoonful of filling in centre of circle and gather edges together, folding and pleating to make a neat join. Twist dough to seal. Place each bun, join downwards on a square of greaseproof paper lightly brushed with sesame oil. Place in steamer, cover and steam for 20 minutes. Serve warm. The cooked buns may be refrigerated overnight and reheated by steaming for 3 minutes before serving.

Barbecued pork buns

Makes: 6-8 buns

Ingredients	Metric	Imperial
Barbecued pork	185 g	6 oz
Peanut oil	2 teaspoons	2 teaspoons
Garlic, crushed	1 small clove	1 small clove
Salt	¼ teaspoon	¼ teaspoon
Cornflour	3 teaspoons	3 teaspoons
Hot water	90 ml	1/3 cup
Soy sauce	2 teaspoons	2 teaspoons
Sesame oil	½ teaspoon	½ teaspoon
Oyster sauce	1 teaspoon	1 teaspoon
Hoi sin sauce	1 teaspoon	1 teaspoon
Sugar	1 teaspoon	1 teaspoon
Red colouring powder	small pinch	small pinch
Dough for steamed buns (See page 116)	1 quantity	1 quantity

Dice pork very small. Heat oil in a pan, add garlic crushed with salt and cook very slowly, not allowing garlic to brown. Add hot water, soy sauce, sesame oil and oyster sauce. Mix cornflour with a tablespoon of cold water and stir in, then cook, stirring until thick and clear. Remove from heat, stir in hoi sin sauce, sugar and red colouring. Cool, then stir in pork.

Mould and steam buns as described (see page 116).

Chicken buns

Makes: 6-8

Ingredients	Metric	Imperial
Chicken breast	1 large	1 large
Cornflour	1 tablespoon	1 tablespoon
Five-spice powder	½ teaspoon	½ teaspoon
Salt	½ teaspoon	½ teaspoon
Peanut oil	2 tablespoons	2 tablespoons
Garlic, bruised	1 clove	1 clove
Chicken stock	250 ml	½ cup
Light soy sauce	1 tablespoon	1 tablespoon
Sesame oil	½ teaspoon	½ teaspoon
Barbecue sauce	1 teaspoon	1 teaspoon
Sugar	1 teaspoon	1 teaspoon
Dough for steamed buns (see page 116)	1 quantity	1 quantity

Bone chicken breast and remove skin. Simmer skin and bone with 1 cup water, a little salt, a slice of ginger and 2 sections of star anise to make the stock needed for this recipe.

Cut breast meat into small dice, dust in half the cornflour mixed with the five-spice powder and salt. Heat peanut oil in a small, deep pan and quickly stir-fry the chicken for 30-40 seconds over high heat. Remove chicken from pan and allow to cool. Pour off oil, leaving about 2 teaspoons. In this gently fry the bruised garlic until it turns golden, then lift out and discard. Add stock, light soy sauce, sesame oil and remaining cornflour mixed smoothly with about 1 tablespoon cold water. Cook and stir until thickened and clear, then remove from heat and add barbecue sauce and sugar. When cool stir in chicken. A little red colouring may be added if liked; but the bottled barbecue sauce is usually sufficient to give the reddish colour this chicken filling should have.

Mould and steam buns as described in recipe on page 116.

Wonton

Wonton are little squares of noodle dough enclosing a savoury meat mixture. They may be deep fried and served as a crisp snack or they may be boiled in soup. Wonton are also known as "Short Soup". Fried Short Soup with Sweet Sour Sauce is a popular dish in restaurants. Wonton wrappers are sold in Chinese grocery stores.

Makes: approximately 40

Ingredients	Metric	Imperial
Dried Chinese mushrooms	6	6
Raw prawns	125 g	4 oz
Finely chopped bamboo shoot	3 tablespoons	3 tablespoons
Shallots	4	4
Minced pork	250 g	8 oz
Salt	1½ teaspoons	1½ teaspoons
Soy sauce	1 tablespoon	1 tablespoon
Sesame oil	1 teaspoon	1 teaspoon
Wonton wrappers	250 g	8 oz
Peanut oil	for deep frying	for deep frying

Soak mushrooms in hot water for 30 minutes, squeeze out excess moisture, trim off and discard stems and chop mushroom caps finely. Shell and de-vein prawns and chop finely. Blanch bamboo shoot in boiling water for 1 minute, drain, then chop finely. Finely chop shallots. Combine all the chopped ingredients with the minced pork and the seasonings.

Put a small amount of filling (about half a teaspoonful) in the centre of each wonton wrapper, moisten edges of dough with water, fold over to a triangle with points slightly overlapping and press together. Then bring the two ends together, dab with a little of the filling mixture where they join and press to seal. When all are made, deep fry a few at a time on medium heat until golden (about 2 minutes). Serve as hors d'oeuvre or as part of a meal with sweet sour sauce.

Dim Sim

Makes: about 2 dozen

Ingredients	Metric	Imperial
Small prawns	500 g	1 lb
Dried Chinese mushrooms	6	6
Canned water chestnuts	6	6
Canned bamboo shoot, chopped	3 tablespoons	3 tablespoons
Shallots, chopped	3	3
Minced pork	250 g	8 oz
Salt	1½ teaspoons	1½ teaspoons
Soy sauce	1 tablespoon	1 tablespoon
Chinese wine or dry sherry, optional	1 tablespoon	1 tablespoon
Sesame oil	1 teaspoon	1 teaspoon
Egg white	1	1
Wonton wrappers	125 g	4 oz

Peel prawns, reserve about 2 dozen for garnish and chop the remainder. Soak mushrooms in hot water 20 minutes, then slice off and discard stems. Chop mushroom caps. Combine all the chopped ingredients with the pork, salt, soy, wine, sesame oil and egg white. Mix well together and place 1 heaped teaspoon of the mixture in the centre of each wonton wrapper. Gather the wrapper around the filling and press it close to give the shape of a little money bag, open at the top. Press a prawn on top of each for decoration. Lightly oil a steamer and place dim sims in a single layer on perforated tray. Cover tightly and steam over boiling water, for 20 minutes. Serve hot or cold with a dipping sauce if liked.

Mandarin pancakes

These delicate crepes are traditionally served with
Peking Duck, but are also used to enclose a variety of fillings
such as egg foo yong, shredded pork or chicken. The filling is
seasoned with a dab of rich flavoured sauce, sprinkled with finely
shredded shallots, then rolled up and eaten as a snack.

Makes: 20 pancakes, serves 4-5

Ingredients	Metric	Imperial
Plain flour	500 g	2 cups
Boiling water	185 ml	¾ cup
Sesame oil	1 tablespoon	1 tablespoon

Measure unsifted flour into bowl. Bring water to the boil and
pour at once onto the flour, stirring with chopsticks or the handle
of a wooden spoon for a few minutes. As soon as it is cool enough
to handle, knead for 10 minutes until the mixture is a soft,
smooth dough. Place dough on a board, cover with a bowl and
let it stand for at least 30 minutes.

Roll dough into a cylindrical shape and cut into 10 slices of
equal size. Keep covered with plastic wrap to prevent drying out.
Take one slice at a time and cut in two equal pieces. Roll each
to a smooth ball, then roll out on a lightly floured board to a
circle about 8 cm (3-inches) in diameter. Brush one circle
lightly with sesame oil, taking it right to the edge of the circle.
Place second circle on first one and roll again, both circles
together this time, until the pancakes are about 15 to 18 cm
(6 or 7-inches) across. They must be very thin. Cover each
pancake as it is made. When they are all rolled out, heat a heavy
frying pan or griddle and place pancakes one at a time on the
ungreased surface. Cook over low heat until pancakes develop
small bubbles. Turn frequently so that they cook on both sides.
A few golden brown spots will appear.

Remove from pan and gently pull the two circles apart. The
sesame oil they were were brushed with makes this quite easy.
Pile the pancakes on a plate and cover tightly or they will dry
out. Pancakes should be soft and pliable, not brittle. To serve,
fold each pancake in quarters.

To reheat, arrange pancakes in a steamer lined with a clean tea
towel, cover and place over simmering water for a minute or two.

Sauces for dipping

Ginger-soy sauce

For any kind of fried seafood or steamed dumplings.

Combine 1 teaspoon very finely grated fresh root ginger with ½ cup light soy sauce.

Chilli-soy sauce

For fried prawns, dim sims, kau che, hot or cold hors d'oeuvre.
Combine 2 tablespoons Chinese chilli sauce and ½ cup soy sauce.

Black bean sherry sauce

Subtle enough for delicate seafood like crabs and scallops.
Rinse and mash 1 tablespoon canned salted black beans, then combine with 3 tablespoons Chinese wine or dry sherry, 1 teaspoon sugar, a few drops of sesame oil.

Black bean garlic sauce

Good with pork or duck.
Rinse and mash 2 tablespoons canned salted black beans, crush 1 small clove garlic, mix beans and garlic with 2 tablespoons each of light soy sauce and Chinese wine or dry sherry.

Plum and barbecue sauce

Serve with roast duck, barbecued pork, Mandarin pancakes.
Combine 6 tablespoons each plum sauce and red barbecue sauce. Stir in ½ teaspoon ginger juice, 2 tablespoons light soy sauce and, if a hotter dip is preferred, 1 teaspoon chilli sauce or to taste.

Sweet sour sauce

Serve with hot hors d'oeuvres or fried won ton.
Make sauce as for Crisp Fried Pork (see page 76) but omit the
vegetables. If liked, stir in a teaspoonful of chilli sauce at the end.

Salt and five-spice mix

Serve with crisp fried chicken, roasted duck or pork.
Mix 2 tablespoons salt with 1 teaspoon five-spice powder.

Roasted pepper and salt mix

Roast 2 tablespoons black peppercorns in a dry pan over medium
heat, shaking pan or stirring, until pepper gives off a pleasant
smell. This takes 4 or 5 minutes. Allow pepper to cool slightly,
then pound with a mortar and pestle and mix with 3 tablespoons
salt. If this is more than you need for one time, store mixture in
an airtight bottle.

Almond jelly

Agar-Agar is a type of seaweed and is sold as a highly refined powder. It makes a jelly with a texture quite different to one made with gelatine, and sets without refrigeration. This sweet, milky, almond-flavoured dessert is popular either by itself or with canned fruits.

Serves: 6-8

Ingredients	Metric	Imperial
Water	1 litre	4 cups
Agar-agar powder	4 teaspoons	4 teaspoons
Sweetened condensed milk	1 x 440 g can	1 x 14 oz can
Almond essence	3 teaspoons	3 teaspoons

Put water into a saucepan, sprinkle agar-agar over and bring to the boil. Boil and stir until agar-agar is dissolved, about 2 minutes. Add condensed milk and almond essence and stir well. Pour into a large shallow glass dish or a large cake tin. Allow to cool and set, then chill. Cut into cubes or diamond shapes and serve by itself or with canned fruits or melon balls.

Lychees and oranges

Canned lychees are a refreshingly light dessert. Serve by themselves or combined with fresh or canned orange or mandarin segments.

Serves: 4-6

Ingredients	Metric	Imperial
Oranges	4	4
Lychees	1 x 565 g can	1 x 1 lb 4 oz can

Peel oranges, removing all the white pith. With a sharp knife cut into segments, discarding all the dividing membrane. Put orange segments into a serving bowl and combine with canned lychees and their syrup. Chill well before serving. If using fresh lychees you will need 500 g (1 lb) of lychees. Peel lychees and put into a bowl.

Make a light sugar syrup by combining 1 cup white sugar with 2 cups water. Dissolve over low heat, boil for 5 minutes, then cool completely before pouring onto the fruit and chilling in the refrigerator.

Black bean pau

These steamed buns with sweet bean paste filling are a between-meal snack rather than a dessert and are eaten by the Chinese much as Western people nibble cookies and candy.

Makes: 8

Ingredients	Metric	Imperial
Dough for steamed buns (see page 116)	1 quantity	1 quantity
Sweet bean paste (Dow Saah)	1 x 255 g can	1 x 9 oz can
Sesame oil for brushing	1 tablespoon	1 tablespoon

Divide dough into 8 equal portions and roll each into a circle about 8 cm (3-inches) in diameter. Put a teaspoonful of bean paste in the centre of each circle and mould and steam buns as described on page 116. Serve warm or at room temperature.

Sweet coconut buns

Makes: 8

Ingredients	Metric	Imperial
Slab sugar	125 g	4 oz
Water	60 ml	¼ cup
Desiccated coconut	1 cup	1 cup
Dough for steamed buns (see page 116)	1 quantity	1 quantity
Sesame oil for brushing	1 tablespoon	1 tablespoon

Put slab sugar and water into a small saucepan and heat gently until sugar is dissolved in the water, then stir in coconut and allow to cool. Mould and steam buns as described on page 116 , using a teaspoonful of the coconut mixture for filling them.

Lotus nut and coconut buns

Makes: 16

Proceed as above, and after stirring in the coconut add the contents of 1 x 227 g (8 oz) can of Lotus Nut Paste. Stir well to combine. You will need a double quantity of dough for this amount of filling. The buns will keep for days in the refrigerator and should be reheated by steaming for 3 minutes to soften them before serving.

1. Kau Che (See page 114)
2. Dim Sim (See page 120)
3. Black Bean Pau (See page 125)
4. Barbecued Pork Buns (See page 117)

Almond biscuits

Makes: approximately 16
Cooking time: 25-30 minutes
Oven temperature: 150-160°C (300°F)

Ingredients	Metric	Imperial
Lard	125 g	4 oz
Castor sugar	½ cup	½ cup
Almond essence	1 teaspoon	1 teaspoon
Yellow food colouring, optional	few drops	few drops
Plain flour	1½ cups	1½ cups
Blanched almonds	8	8
Egg yolk	1	1
Water	1 tablespoon	1 tablespoon

Soften lard to room temperature and beat lard and sugar together until soft and creamy. Add almond essence and, if liked, a little yellow colouring. Add the unsifted flour gradually, stirring well to combine. After adding the last of the flour it will be necessary to work the mixture with the hand, but it will still be of a crumbly consistency.

Take level tablespoons of the dough and shape into flat round cakes about 5 cm (2-inches) in diameter. Edges of cakes will have little cracks in them. Place on a well greased baking tray. Put almonds in a small pan with a little cold water, bring to the boil, drain. Split almonds in two. Press half an almond in the centre of each biscuit. Beat egg yolk with water and brush tops of biscuits.

Bake in a slow oven for 30 minutes or until pale golden. Cool slightly on tray, then carefully lift on to wire rack, using a spatula. When cold, store airtight.

Oriental fruit basket

Serves: 6-8

Take a medium sized watermelon and cut off the top third. With a melon baller scoop out melon flesh, discarding seeds. Combine melon balls with any of the following: canned lychees, longans, loquats, mandarin segments. Mix with some of the syrup from the cans. Cover and chill at least 3 hours. If liked, a few canned or bottled chow chow preserves may be added. Before serving arrange fruits in the watermelon shell and spoon some of the syrup over.

Oriental Fruit Basket (See page 129)

GLOSSARY OF INGREDIENTS

Agar-agar: A setting agent obtained from seaweed. Available in powder form from chemists or in packets from Chinese grocery stores. Also sold in strands.

Bamboo Shoot: Sold in cans either water-packed or braized. Unless otherwise stated, the recipes in this book call for the water-packed variety. After opening can, store in a bowl of fresh water in the refrigerator, replacing water daily, for up to 10 days.

Barbecue Sauce: A reddish sauce, very salty and at the same time sweet. Use as a dip or as an ingredient in barbecue marinades. Keeps indefinitely in covered jar.

Bean Sprouts: Green mung beans are used for bean sprouts. They are sold fresh in most Chinese stores and in certain supermarkets and health food stores. The canned variety are not recommended. Substitute thinly sliced celery for crunchy texture, though flavour is different. Fresh bean sprouts may be stored in refrigerator for a week in plastic bag. Or cover with water and change water daily.

Black Beans Salted: Make from soy beans, heavily salted and preserved in cans. Similar to salted yellow beans. Rinse before using to prevent over-salting in recipes. Substitute extra soy sauce. Store in covered container in refrigerator after opening for 6 months or longer, adding a little peanut oil if top seems to dry out.

Chilli Sauce: Chinese chilli sauce is different to other chilli sauce. Substitute Tabasco or other hot pepper sauce, not one of the sweet chilli sauces. Keeps indefinitely.

Chinese Mushrooms: These dried mushrooms are sold by weight. They are expensive but add incomparable flavour. Do not substitute fresh mushrooms or dried Continental mushrooms. Soak in hot water for 30 minutes before cooking. Stems and soaking water may be saved for flavouring stock.

Chinese parsley also known as **Fresh Coriander:** This dark green pungent herb is widely used in Chinese cooking. Do not use more than the amount stated as it is likely to overpower other flavours. Store in tightly closed plastic bags in refrigerator for 2 weeks.

Chinese Sausages: Dried sausages filled only with spiced lean and fat pork, which will keep without refrigeration. Steam for 10 minutes until soft and plump, cut in thin slices to serve or include in dishes.

Chow Chow Preserves: A mixture of fruits and vegetables preserved in a heavy syrup flavoured by the ginger which is one of the ingredients. Sold in cans or jars and keeps indefinitely in refrigerator.

Five-spice powder: A combination of ground anise, fennel, cinnamon, cloves and Szechuan pepper, it gives distinctive flavour in cooking and is also used as a dip, combined with salt.

Garlic: Use fresh garlic in Chinese food, dried garlic flakes or powder are too pungent. In some instances the garlic clove is fried in the oil, then lifted out and discarded, leaving just a delicate flavour.

Ginger root: A basic seasoning in Chinese food. Buy fresh root ginger from Chinese food shops, greengrocers, supermarkets. Store by freezing in a plastic bag; peeling and bottling in a jar of dry sherry (store in refrigerator); or burying in moist soil and watering frequently. Dig up a piece as needed, replace remaining ginger root in soil and keep moist. If you are able to buy it frequently, store in the crisper section of the refrigerator where it will keep fresh for about 3 weeks. Ginger is also available sliced in cans and this is the best substitute for fresh ginger. Do not use powdered ginger as a substitute.

Hoi sin Sauce: A sweet, spicy, reddish brown sauce of thick pouring consistency made from soy beans, garlic, spices. Used in barbecued pork dishes and as a dip. Keep in well covered jar. Keeps indefinitely.

Lily Buds: Also known as "golden needles" or lotus buds, these dried golden buds, long and narrow, have a very delicate flavour and are said to be very nutritious. Soak for half an hour or longer in hot water. Cut in half crossways for easier eating.

Lotus Nut Paste: A sweet paste made from lotus nuts and sugar, used as a filling in Chinese sweetmeats.

Lotus Root: Sometimes available fresh. Peel, cut into slices and use as directed. Dried lotus root must be soaked at least 20 minutes in hot water with a little lemon juice added to preserve whiteness. Canned lotus root is readily available and may be stored in the refrigerator for a few days once opened.

Monosodium Glutamate: White crystals rather like Epsom salts in appearance. An extract of grains and vegetables with no flavour of its own but it acts as a catalyst on the taste buds to enhance other flavours. If food is of good quality and cleverly seasoned, it is not necessary to use this additive. Though some cooks use it as universally as soy sauce in Chinese cooking, I prefer not to.

Mushrooms, Chinese dried: See under Chinese Mushrooms.

Oyster Sauce: Adds delicate flavour to all kinds of dishes. Made from oysters cooked in soy sauce and brine, this thick brown sauce keeps indefinitely once opened.

Parsley, Chinese: See Chinese Parsley.

Plum Sauce: A spicy, chutney-like sweet, hot sauce made from plums, chillies, vinegar, spices and sugar. Use as a dip. Keeps indefinitely in covered jar.

Preserved Melon Shreds: Thin shreds of melon preserved in a ginger-flavoured syrup. Use in small quantities to garnish. Substitute finely shredded chow chow preserves. Keeps indefinitely in jar.

Red Bean Paste: A thick, sweet paste made from red soy beans and used in barbecue type dishes.

Red Colouring Powder: A brilliant red powder sold in Chinese stores and used very sparingly to give the distinctive colour seen in barbecued pork. Substitute red food colouring.

Sausages, Chinese: See under Chinese Sausages.

Sesame oil: In Chinese cooking, this oil is extracted from toasted sesame seeds, giving it a rich amber colour and totally different flavour from the lighter sesame oil sometimes sold in health stores. For the recipes in this book, purchase sesame oil from Chinese stores. Use in small quantities for flavouring, not as a cooking medium.

Sesame Paste: Ground sesame seeds form a thick paste similar to peanut butter. Middle Eastern stores sell a sesame paste known as "tahini" but this is made with raw sesame seeds and is white and slightly bitter, whereas the Chinese version is made with toasted sesame seeds and is brown and nutty. Substitute a similar amount of smooth peanut butter with sesame oil added for flavour. Sold in cans or jars, keeps indefinitely after opening.

Shallots: (Spring onions) The member of the onion family known as a shallot in Australia is correctly called a spring onion almost everywhere else. Use the straight, slender onions without large, well developed bulbs.

Slab Sugar: A pale brown sugar in tablet form, it has distinctive flavour and is used for sweetening fillings for Chinese buns and biscuits.

Snow Peas: Also known as Sugar Peas. Sold fresh in season, these are mainly a speciality of Chinese market gardeners but large seed companies now sell the seeds in packets under the name of Sugar Peas. They are never cooked for longer than a minute or two and are eaten pod and all. The French name for them is mange-tout. They are sometimes available frozen, but lack the delightful crispness of the fresh peas. Store fresh snow peas for a few days in a plastic bag or in a bowl of water in the refrigerator.

Soy Sauce: Indispensable in Chinese cooking, this versatile sauce enhances the flavour of every basic ingredient in a dish. Different grades are available. Dark soy sauce is used in most instances, but light soy is used when cooking chicken or seafood, or in soups where the delicate colour of the dish must be preserved. Keeps indefinitely.

Spring Roll Wrappers: Thin, white sheets of pastry sold in plastic packets. Usually frozen. Unused wrappers may be refrozen. Large wonton wrappers may not be substituted.

Star Anise: One of the prettiest seed pods, it looks like a reddish brown, eight-petalled flower. Used in stocks or master sauces for red-cooked dishes, it imparts a licorice flavour.

Straw Mushrooms: Unlike dried mushrooms with their strong flavour, these mushrooms are as delicately flavoured as champignons. They are shrouded in their own little "tent" which envelopes the stalk and cap with a thin skin. Sold in cans.

Sweet Bean Paste: Made from soy beans and sugar, this paste, known as Dow Saah, is used in sweet steamed buns or New Year Doughnuts.

Walnuts: Who but the Chinese would have the patience to peel walnut kernels? Peeled walnuts are sold by weight in Chinese grocery stores and are perfect for using in fried dishes, as the thin skin which turns bitter through cooking has been removed. If peeled walnuts are not available, use the canned, salted walnuts also sold in Chinese stores. These do not need further cooking.

Water Chestnuts: Sometimes available fresh, the brownish black skin must be peeled away with a sharp knife, leaving the crisp, slightly sweet kernel. Available in cans, already peeled. After opening, store in water in refrigerator for a week or 10 days, changing water daily.

Wheat corn paste: Thick, clear sweet syrup, pale golden in colour, used in barbecued dishes. Measure with a heated spoon. Keeps indefinitely. Honey may be substituted.

Wonton Wrappers: Small squares of fresh noodle dough bought from Chinese stores. Refrigerate, well wrapped in plastic, for a week. Approximately 45 to the half pound.

Wood Fungus: Sold by weight, wood fungus in its dry state looks like greyish black pieces of paper. Soaked in hot water for 10 minutes it swells to translucent brown shapes like curved clouds or a rather prettily shaped ear. Hence the name it is sometimes known by, "cloud ear" fungus. Adds no flavour but distinctive, crunchy texture. Keeps indefinitely.

Index

A.
Abalone chow mein and chicken 104
Abalone with Szechwan style pork 82
Almond biscuits 129
Almond Jelly 124
Asparagus and chicken soup 21

B.
Bamboo shoot with pork and prawn ball
  soup 24
Bamboo shoot with prawn balls 33
Bamboo shoot with young corn cobs and
  snow peas in red sauce 87
Barbecue style roast duck 61
Barbecued pork 79
Barbecued pork buns 117
Barbecued pork spareribs 78
Basic chicken stock 16
Basic fish stock 17
Bean curd braised in oyster sauce 86
Bean curd with crab sauce 85
Bean sprouts with broccoli and water
  chestnuts 86
Bean sprouts with shredded beef and
  walnuts 69
BEEF AND PORK 65
Beef
  braised with noodles 103
  fillet in black bean sauce 66
  fried and long beans 71
  red cooked 67
  shredded five-spice with broccoli 68
  shredded with bean sprouts and
    walnuts 69
  stir-fried and vegetables in oyster
    sauce 70
  with lotus root 72
Black bean
  garlic sauce 122
  pau 125
  sauce, chicken in 59
  sauce with beef fillet 66
  sauce with prawns and mushrooms 35
  sherry sauce 122
Biscuits, almond 129
Boiled noodles 99
Boiled rice 95
Braised
  chicken and mushrooms with Chinese
    parsley 60
  duck with green peas and cashew
    nuts 63
  duck with lily buds and mushrooms 62
  mushrooms 90
  noodles with chicken 102
  pork balls and mushrooms 83
  pork with noodles 75
Broccoli, bean sprouts and water
  chestnuts 86
Broccoli with shredded five spice
  beef 68
Buns
  black bean pau 125
  chicken 118
  coconut and lotus nut 126
  coconut sweet 126
  dough for steamed 116
  lotus nut and coconut 126
  pork (barbecued) 117
  sweet coconut 126
Butterfly prawns 108

C.
Cabbage and pork soup 23
Cabbage, mustard and stir-fried prawns 34
Cashew nuts with braised duck and
  green peas 63
Cellophane or bean starch noodles 94
Chicken
  and abalone chow mein 104
  and almonds with straw mushrooms 58
  and asparagus soup 21
  braised with mushrooms and Chinese
    parsley 60
  buns 118
  in black bean sauce 59
  red cooked 54
  soup, whole 18
  spiced and oven roasted 57
  stock, basic 16
  velvet and sweet corn soup 22
Chilli-soy sauce 122
Chinese chopper 13
Chinese parsley with chicken and
  mushrooms 60
Chow mein combination 101
Combination long soup 30
Combination soup 29
Conjee 96
Corn cobs, young, and snow peas with
  bamboo shoot in red sauce 87
Corn cobs, young, and snow peas with
  cucumber 88
Crab
  and egg soup 26
  meat rolls 115
  omelette 52
  sauce with bean curd 85
Crisp fried noodles 100
Crisp fried pork with sweet sour sauce 76
Crisp skin fish with sweet sour sauce 44
Cucumber with young corn cobs and
  snow peas 88

D.
Dim sim 120
Dipping sauces 122
Dough for steamed buns 116
Duck
  barbecue style 61
  braised with green peas and cashew
    nuts 63
  braised with lily buds and mushrooms
    62
  roast Szechwanese style 64
Dumplings pork 111

E.
Egg and poultry 49
Egg(s)
  and crab soup 26
  flower soup 25
  foo yong with meat 53
  foo yong with prawns 53

133

foo yong with sprouts 53
marbled tea 113
noodles 94
roll 50
roll with prawn filling 51

F.
Fillet of beef in black bean sauce 66
Fish (see also under specific variety
  headings)
  crisp skin, with sweet sour sauce 44
  fried with vegetables 46
  steamed with mushroom sauce 48
  stock, basic 17
Five-spice, shredded beef with
  broccoli 68
Foo yong, eggs with meat 53
Foo yong, egg with prawns 53
Foo yong, eggs with sprouts 53
Fried beef and long beans 71
Fried fish with vegetables 46
Fried prawn balls with snow peas 36
Fried prawns with ginger 47
Fruit basket, oriental 129
Fruit, lychees and oranges 124

G.
Ginger-soy sauce 122
Ginger with fried prawns 47
GLOSSARY OF INGREDIENTS 130-2
Gow jee or Kau che 114
GUIDE TO WEIGHTS AND
  MEASURES 9

H.
Heavenly braised vegetables 89
Hors d'oeuvres, hot 106

I.
INTRODUCTION 8

J.
Jelly, almond 124

K.
Kau che or gow jee 114
Kitchen aids 12-14

L.
Lily buds, with braised duck and
  mushrooms 62
Long beans and fried beef 71
Long soup, combination 30
Long soup with king prawns 31
Lotus nut and coconut buns 126
Lotus root with beef 72
Lychees and oranges 124

M.
Mandarin pancakes 121
Marbled tea eggs 113
Meat: (See under specific headings)
Meat with eggs foo yong 53
Miniature scallop rolls 112
Mixed braised vegetables 88
Mixed fried rice 99

Mushroom(s)
  and prawn soup 27
  and prawns in black bean sauce 35
  braised 90
  sauce with steamed fish 48
  with braised duck and lily buds 62
  with braised pork balls 83
  with chicken and Chinese parsley 60
Mustard cabbage and stir-fried prawns 34

N.
Noodles
  and rice 93
  boiled 99
  braised with chicken 102
  cellophane or bean starch 94
  egg 94
  rice 94
  soft fried 100
  with braised beef 103
  with braised pork 75

O.
Omelette, crab 52
Oranges and lychees 124
Oriental fruit basket 129
Oven roasted spiced chicken 57
Oyster sauce with braised bean curd 86
Oyster sauce, with stir fried beef and
  vegetables 70

P
Pancakes, Mandarin 121
Pasta: (see under specific headings)
Pastry, dim sim 120
Pastry, wonton 119
Peas with braised duck and cashew
  nuts 63
Plum and barbecue sauce 123
Pork
  and beef 65
  and cabbage soup 23
  and prawn ball soup with bamboo
    shoot 24
  balls, braised with mushrooms 83
  barbecued 79
  barbecued spareribs 78
  braised with noodles 75
  buns, barbecued 117
  crisp fried with sweet sour sauce 76
  dumplings 111
  with abalone, Szechwan style 82
  spring rolls 113
POULTRY AND EGGS 49
Prawn(s)
  and mushroom soup 27
  and mushrooms in black bean sauce 35
  and pork ball soup with bamboo
    shoot 24
  balls, fried, with snow peas 36
  balls with bamboo shoots 33
  butterfly 108
  filling, egg roll 51
  fried with ginger 47
  king, with long soup 31
  stir-fried and mustard cabbage 34
  toast 107
  with eggs foo yong 53

R.
Red cooked beef 67
Red cooked chicken 54
Red sauce with young corn cobs, snow
 peas and bamboo shoot 87
Rice
 and noodles 93
 boiled 95
 boiled savoury 95
 conjee 96
 fried mixed 99
 fried, simple 97
 fried vegetarian 98
 noodles 94
 vermicelli 94
Roast duck, Szechwanese style 64
Roasted pepper and salt mix 123
Roll egg 50
Roll, egg with prawn filling 51
SAUCES 105
 black bean garlic 122
 black bean sherry 122
 black bean with beef fillet 66
 black bean with chicken 59
 black bean with prawns and
  mushrooms 35
 chilli-soy 122
 for dipping 122
 garlic, black bean 122
 ginger soy 122
 mushroom, with steamed fish 48
 oyster with braised bean curd 86
 oyster with stir-fried beef and
  vegetables 70
 plum and barbecue 122
 red, with young corn cobs, snow peas
  and bamboo shoot 87
 roasted pepper and salt mix 123
 salt and five-spice mix 123
 sweet sour 123
 sweet sour with crisp fried pork 76
 sweet sour, with crisp skin fish 44
Savoury boiled rice 95
Scallop rolls, miniature 112
Scallops with snow peas 39
SEAFOOD 32 (see also under specific
 headings)
Short soup with vegetables 28
Short soup (wonton soup) 28
Shredded beef with bean sprouts and
 walnuts 69
Shredded five-spice beef with broccoli
 68
Simple fried rice 97
SNACKS, SAUCES AND SWEETS 105
Snow peas with fried prawn balls 36
Snow peas with scallops 39
Snow peas with young corn cobs and
 bamboo shoot in red sauce 87
Snow peas and young corn cobs with
 cucumber 88
Soft fried noodles 100
SOUPS
 chicken and asparagus 21
 chicken velvet and sweet corn 22
 combination 29
 combination long 30

crab and egg 26
egg flower 25
long, with king prawns 31
mushroom and prawn 27
pork and cabbage 23
pork and prawn ball with bamboo
 shoot 24
short with vegetables 28
short (wonton) 28
whole chicken 18
Spareribs, barbecued pork 78
Spring rolls, crab meat 115
Spring rolls, miniature scallop 112
Spring rolls, pork 113
Sprouts with eggs foo yong 53
Steamed fish with mushroom sauce 48
Steamers 13
Stir-fried beef and vegetables in oyster
 sauce 70
Stir-fried prawns and mustard cabbage
 34
Stock, basic chicken 16
Stock, basic fish 17
Straw mushrooms with chicken and
 almonds 58
Sweet coconut buns 126
Sweet sour sauce 123
Sweet sour sauce with crisp fried pork 76
Sweet sour sauce with crisp skin fish 44
Sweetcorn and chicken velvet soup 22
SWEETS 105
Szechwan style pork with abalone 82
Szechwanese style, roast duck 64

T.
Toast, prawn 107
To season your wok 12

U.
Utensils for Chinese cooking 12

V.
Vegetables 84 (see also under specific
 headings)
 heavenly braised 89
 mixed braised 88
 with fried fish 46
 with stir-fried beef in oyster sauce 70
Vegetarian fried rice 98
Vermicelli rice 94

W.
Walnuts with shredded beef and bean
 sprouts 69
Water chestnuts with broccoli and
 bean sprouts 86
WEIGHTS AND MEASURES GUIDE 9
Whole chicken soup 18
Wonton 119
Wonton soup (short soup) 28

Y.
Young corn cobs and snow peas with
 bamboo shoot in red sauce 87
Young corn cobs and snow peas with
 cucumber 88